YOU AND YOUR BODY

What causes spots?
Why do you put on weight?
What is dandruff?
When is it allowed to have sex?

You and Your Body tells you all you want to know about your body — how it works, what can go wrong, how it changes. There are chapters on General Health, Skin Problems, Diet, Food and Growth, Drugs and Medicines, Personality, Relationships and Mental Health, Sex, Serious Illnesses, and a useful section on the Health Services, with a reference section. Everything is explained in a clear, candid and straightforward manner, with diagrams where necessary — the ideal reference book for people of ten and over.

YOU AND YOUR BODY

David Keable-Elliott

Beaver Books

A Beaver Book
Published by Arrow Books Limited
17–21 Conway Street, London W1P 6JD

A division of the Hutchinson Publishing Group
London Melbourne Sydney Auckland Johannesburg
and agencies throughout the world

First published in 1983 by Hamish Hamilton Children's Books
Beaver edition 1984

© Copyright text David Keable-Elliot © 1983
© Copyright illustrations Hamish Hamilton Children's Books © 1983

This book is sold subject to the condition that it shall not, by way of trade or otherwise, be lent, resold, hired out, or otherwise circulated without the publisher's prior consent in any form of binding or cover other than that in which it is published and without a similar condition including this condition being imposed on the subsequent purchaser.

Printed and bound in Great Britain by
Cox & Wyman Ltd, Reading

ISBN 0 09 937350 5

Contents

	Introduction	7
One	**GENERAL HEALTH**	9
Two	**SKIN PROBLEMS**	61
Three	**DIET, FOOD AND GROWTH**	79
Four	**DRUGS AND MEDICINES**	91
Five	**PERSONALITY, RELATIONSHIPS AND MENTAL HEALTH**	105
Six	**SEX**	121
Seven	**SERIOUS ILLNESSES**	153
Eight	**HEALTH SERVICES**	171
	Helpful organisations	181
	Further reading	183
	Index	185

I would like to acknowledge the debt I owe to my editor Christine Sandeman. Without her encouragement and guidance through the long days of preparation, this book would never have been completed.

I would also like to thank Anne Pearson and Mary Thompson for their helpful comments.

Introduction

This book is a practical guide to the human body. It gives a frank description of a young person's mental, physical and emotional development, advice on health problems he or she may encounter, and some of the more common illnesses that older friends or relatives may experience. In short, it attempts to answer all those questions which a young person would like to have answered, but may not dare to ask.

The book is divided into eight chapters, all of which (bar 'Sex') are subdivided alphabetically into separate sections. It starts with a chapter on 'General health', which discusses common symptoms and illnesses. This is followed by more specialist chapters, each of which deal with important facets of a young person's life. 'Skin problems', 'Diet, food and growth', 'Drugs and medicines', and 'Personality, relationships and mental health' are all made up of fairly short sections which can be used for reference or just read straight through. Chapter six, 'Sex', gives information on all aspects of sex and is of necessity arranged in logical sequence. The two remaining chapters give the young reader valuable information on serious health problems which may be affecting their relatives, or which they have heard about through the media, and on those areas of the health service which they are most likely to come into contact with.

Throughout the book, there is extensive cross-referencing, which operates both between and within chapters. Words in bold type indicate the start of a subsection or a medical term which, though likely to be of interest to the young reader, does not justify a section to itself. At the end of the book there is a wide-ranging reading list, a selection of useful organisations and a comprehensive index.

David Keable-Elliott
October, 1982

1
General Health

ABSCESS

An abscess is a spot of infection that causes pus to collect. Small abscesses on the skin are called boils or carbuncles (see p. 65). They heal up quickly once they have burst.

Abscesses inside the body are more serious and often require an operation to lay open the abscess and clean out the infection.

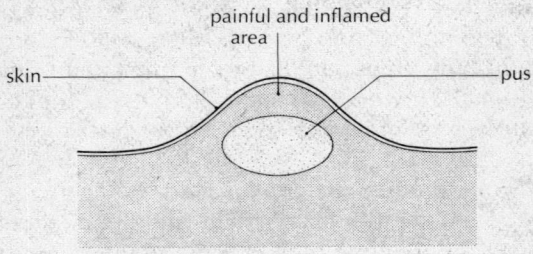

A boil (abscess under the skin)

ALLERGY

To be allergic to something means that when you touch, eat or inhale that thing you experience unpleasant symptoms as a result. For example, if you are allergic to the nickel in metal, you will develop a rash whenever you wear a watchstrap or piece of jewellery with nickel in it.

It is possible to be allergic to almost anything. Every day you eat, touch and smell millions of different substances, and usually your body is very good at sorting out which are harmful and which are harmless. It protects itself from harmful things by neutralising small amounts of poison in the food you eat and fighting off germs which might cause disease. You do not even notice this process.

But with an allergic reaction, your body over-reacts and tries to fight off something that is actually harmless. The rash which appears under your metal watchstrap shows that your body is trying to fight off the nickel in the metal.

Different types of allergy
Different types of allergy are called by different names. You may get allergic rashes to tablets, medicines or certain foods, or from touching rubber gloves, cosmetics or soaps. Hay fever (see p. 38) and sometimes asthma (see WHEEZING, p. 59) are caused by an allergy to pollens and grasses. Allergies to insect bites and to some drugs can lead to an unpleasant swelling of the face. However, all these allergic reactions can be controlled by medicines which your doctor will give you.

If your mother or father suffers from any sort of allergy you are more likely to be allergic to something yourself. But allergies are not catching, and what causes an allergic reaction in one person will probably not have a similar effect on another.

Allergies to foods
It is likely that allergies to foods cause some of the mild headaches and stomach upsets that many people suffer from. But it is often difficult to pin down exactly what is causing the trouble.

Some people get quite bad reactions to one particular food, with severe headaches (see MIGRAINE, p. 46), extensive skin rashes or other symptoms. In these cases the culprit can usually be identified quite easily; it is often a food like mushrooms, eggs or shellfish.

Coeliac disease People suffering from this disease are allergic to the gluten in wheat flour. They must therefore avoid all foods containing wheat. This is difficult since so many foods have wheat in them — bread, pastry, cereals and batter are just some of the most common.

ANAEMIA

If you are anaemic you may find that you often feel tired or get short of breath. (But do remember that many other things can cause these symptoms.) You feel like this because your blood is thinner than normal.

Anaemia can develop if you have lost a lot of blood (a lot of blood is several pints, not just the amount from an average cut or a twenty-minute nosebleed), or as a result of a bad infection or disease.

Girls sometimes become anaemic if their periods are very heavy for six months or more. If clots regularly appear in their period loss they should check with their doctor that all is well. As iron tablets help this type of anaemia, you may be given a course of these tablets.

Iron tablets are also often given to pregnant girls since pregnancy can bring on anaemia.

Too much iron is bad for you, so the tablets should only be taken if prescribed by a doctor. Iron tablets often look like sweets so they should be kept well out of the reach of young children.

A doctor can find out if you are anaemic by doing a blood test to check the thickness of your blood. This test can detect even mild anaemia.

APPENDICITIS

The appendix is a small pouch that is attached to the last part of the intestines. It does not perform any useful function, but if it becomes infected, forming an abscess (see p. 9) appendicitis will result.

If you have appendicitis you feel sick and ill and your stomach hurts. Usually, your doctor will know that you have appendicitis, but sometimes he cannot be absolutely sure and he may wait for a few hours to see if the pain gets better. But if the pain is very bad you will almost certainly have an operation straightaway to remove the appendix. It is safer to have the operation than risk waiting for too long and having a burst appendix.

Of course, most stomach pains are not appendicitis. Indigestion (see p. 39) and constipation (see p. 22) both cause nasty pains and are quite common, especially in young people.

The appendix operation usually means being in hospital for about seven days, and off school or work for another three weeks after that. If you have had a burst appendix you may feel quite weak for several months. You will have a small scar on the right-hand side of your lower abdomen to remind you of the operation.

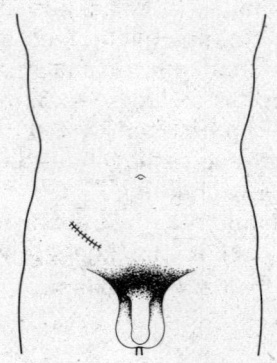

The scar of an appendix operation

ARTHRITIS (see p. 155 for other types of arthritis)

Arthritis is a condition which causes pain in the joints. There are many different types of arthritis, though there are relatively few which affect young people. Remember that infections such as flu, german measles and tonsilitis can also produce pains in the joints.

All joints may become infected. Unless the infection is treated quickly, it can damage the joint. So if a joint of yours becomes suddenly painful and swollen, visit a doctor without delay.

Some types of arthritis in young people affect mainly one set of joints. A few of these types are mentioned below:

The back

Ankylosing spondylitis is an arthritis of the lower back, making it stiff and painful. The condition improves as you get older, but it is very important that you follow your doctor's advice about exercise. Otherwise, the back trouble could become permanent.

Scheuermanns disease, **spinal osteochondritis** Neither of these two diseases is very serious and will clear up as you get older. It is important to keep a good posture and to avoid violent exercise that strains the back.

The hip

Several conditions can affect the hip joint and cause a limp. The long thigh bone ends at the hip in a round ball which fits securely into a socket in the hip bone. If, when a baby is born, the ball does not fit properly into the socket, the baby will have a dislocated hip. This is almost always treatable, but if it is not treated the child may grow up with a limp.

Irritable hip A common cause for a sudden limp in a young person is an irritable hip. This will get better of its own accord, usually in a few days, but needs to be

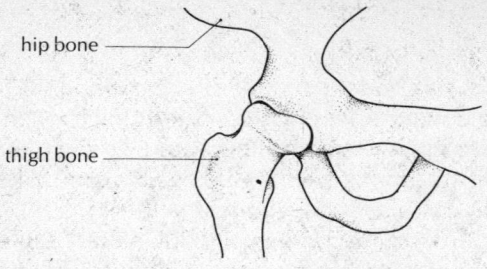

The bones of the hip joint

distinguished from the other much rarer conditions mentioned below.

Perthes disease With this disease the growing end of the thigh-bone becomes fragile and the person affected has to take good care of him or herself for a year or two until the bone regains its strength.

Slipped epiphysis The growing end of the thigh-bone slips slightly out of place and may need treatment to correct. After a couple of years the bone regains its strength.

The knee

Almost all knee injuries damage the ligaments which hold the knee together. The ligaments will heal themselves, but they need time and patience. Cartilage injuries are more serious and take longer to clear up (cartilage is the substance which makes up the smooth surface of the knee joint).

There are a number of rare types of arthritis which affect the knee, and which need treatment from a hospital doctor who specialises in bone diseases. Most of these conditions improve over several years, though they may interfere with sporting activities.

ASTHMA (see WHEEZING, p. 59)

BACK TROUBLE

Many people suffer from back pain, which is almost always brought on by straining the back over a long period of time. If your posture is bad, whether you are sitting, standing or lifting, you are more likely to have trouble with your back later on. Often by the time the pain starts, the damage has been done. The ligaments (strong bands of gristle that hold the backbones together) have started to stretch, and the little joints between the bones of the back have started to become worn and stiff.

Slipped disc

Disc trouble is more serious. If you have a slipped disc, one of the soft shock-absorbers that fit between the vertebrae (bones of the spine) has become squashed and slipped out of place. It may even slip far enough out of place to need an operation to repair the damage, though this is not usual.

BAD BREATH

Bad breath (or halitosis) is caused by harmless, but smelly germs growing inside the mouth. Though they are easily killed, they tend to come back unless you pay special attention to keeping your mouth clean.

Brushing your teeth regularly and, if necessary, using an antiseptic gargle will control most attacks of bad breath. Visit a dentist so that he can check that there is no infection in the teeth or gums causing the trouble.

If a friend of yours has bad breath, they may not notice it, so it would be kind to tell them — tactfully of course!

BEDWETTING

Bedwetting is a problem which nobody talks about, but which a large number of people have at one time or another. It is also something which your doctor will be used to sorting out, so try not to be embarrassed to talk to him or her about it.

If the bedwetting has been going on for many years, it is very unlikely that there is any particular reason for it. But if the problem has only just started, an attack of cystitis (see p. 25) or some other bodily upset could be to blame. Your doctor will probably do one or two simple tests to find out if there is an obvious physical cause.

You and your doctor will then decide on the way to tackle the problem. An easy first step is to avoid drinking any fluid last thing at night and to make sure you go to the lavatory at this time. Also, it often helps to keep a diary to record successful nights. If these simple measures do not work, tablets or alarm bell systems (which wake you up when you wet the bed) will probably clear up the trouble.

Bedwetting is not difficult to cure. Often the most difficult thing is asking for help.

BLEEDING (see also CIRCULATION, p. 20, and CUTS, p. 24)

Bleeding, except during a girl's period, is a sign of injury or damage. Internal damage, which causes bleeding, is usually a result of infection. For example, blood in the urine may be caused by a bruise on the kidney, though it is more likely to be the result of cystitis (see p. 25). If you notice any bleeding, for which there is no obvious cause, it is important you go to a doctor for a check-up.

Nosebleeds

Nosebleeds are very common. They occur when the small group of blood vessels near the surface of the skin inside the nose are bruised or damaged in some way. For example, a cold, or a light thump on the nose may result in broken blood vessels. Nosebleeds are especially likely if you pick your nose.

The first thing to do when you have a nosebleed is to keep calm. However much blood you seem to be losing, there is no risk of bleeding to death! Sit forward and breathe through your mouth. Avoid blowing your nose because this will dislodge the clot which is forming and which will stop the bleeding. Cooling the nose with a flannel wrapped in ice often helps. Be patient! It may take a little time to stop.

If you have a lot of nosebleeds, it is possible to have the bleeding point cauterised (sealed off) and the problem solved. Your doctor will be able to advise you about this.

BOIL (see p. 65)

BRONCHITIS

Bronchitis is the medical name for a type of infection in the lungs (see p. 43). It often comes on as a nasty cough after a bad cold.

If the lungs have been damaged over a long period of time – by smoking, for instance – they become especially liable to bronchitis. Frequent attacks of bronchitis may result in chronic bronchitis. The sufferer will then cough up phlegm and quickly become short of breath.

Bronchitis can be helped by antibiotics but not actually cured. Lung transplants are not possible, so if you are even slightly prone to chesty infections, you should not smoke.

BRUISING

Bruises are caused by damage and bleeding under the skin and they usually take only a few days to clear up. A compress, either hot or cold, will ease the discomfort, but otherwise there is little else you can do.

A black eye is a bruise around the eye. It owes its colourful appearance to the looseness of the skin in this area. A flannel wrapped in ice eases the pain just as effectively as a raw steak!

Haemophilia This is a disease caused by the blood clotting too slowly so that bruises appear very easily. It runs in families and is only inherited by boys. Although it is not curable, modern treatments enable even the worst affected person to lead an active life.

Henoch-schoenlein purpura Bruising which appears for no apparent reason is a symptom of this skin disease. It gets better of its own accord, but needs watching by a doctor to ensure that there are no complications. Other causes of such bruising are rarer and a doctor should be consulted.

BUNIONS

A bunion is a painful lump at the side of the big toe. It is often the result of wearing a series of badly-fitting shoes which have pushed the toes out of line. An operation can be done to straighten the toes, but the discomfort from the bunion may not be sufficient to justify the inconvenience of a hospital stay. Well-fitting shoes and a protective pad may be enough to solve the problem.

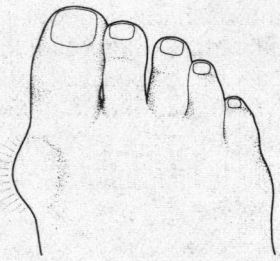

A bunion

BURNS

Depending on how much of you is burnt, a burn may be merely uncomfortable or actually life-threatening.

Obviously, the severity of the burn depends on how hot the burning material was.

Fortunately, most household scalds and burns are not too serious. Whatever the cause, it is very important to cool the burnt skin as quickly as possible. In the home this is best done by running cold water over the affected area.

Unless the skin is broken or badly blistered, no dressing is needed. Just soothe the area with a mild antiseptic cream. Blisters should not be popped – they protect the lower layers of skin from infection. If the burnt skin is broken or blistered, it is best to get medical attention. Never put a sticky plaster on a burn.

Deep burns

Deep burns, especially those caused by electrical appliances or prolonged contact with heat, will completely destroy an area of skin. The skin does not recover quickly and an operation, called skin grafting, is usually needed to repair the damaged area. This operation leaves a scar.

Acids and other chemicals often cause deep burns unless the chemical is washed off very quickly. You should always take care not to touch powerful chemicals that might burn, but if you have to handle such substances, make sure you know what to do in the event of an accident.

CHICKENPOX

Chickenpox is a mild illness which most children catch when they are quite young.

The itchy spots can be soothed with calamine lotion and the child is infectious until the spots have dried up (usually about ten days). You can only have chickenpox once.

Shingles

The bug which causes chickenpox can also cause shingles later on in life. Shingles gives you a bad chickenpox rash, but only on a small part of the body. This rash can be quite painful.

CIRCULATION

Blood is pumped around the body from the heart. You can feel your heart pumping if you press one finger into the space between the ribs, just below your left nipple.

The blood is pushed out along the arteries and then collected in veins and taken back to the heart. At the wrist you can feel the artery pulsing with each beat of the heart. This is the main artery taking blood to the fingers. If you hang your arm down, you can see the veins in your forearm filling out. These veins are taking blood back to the heart from where it will be pumped out again.

Feel your pulse beating at your wrist, elbow, neck, under your ribs and at your groin

The circulating blood keeps the different parts of the body alive. If a tight bandage (a tourniquet) is tied around the arm, the blood flow will be blocked. After about twenty minutes the fingers will start to die. If you are bleeding heavily and want to control the loss of blood, it is far safer to press firmly on the bleeding spot than to apply a tourniquet.

COLDS

Colds are caused by viral infection (see INFECTION, p. 41). There are many different types of virus and, as yet, there is no cure for them. Most children have a few colds every year, but as the child gets older he or she becomes less liable to infections. The average adult has only one or two colds a year.

The symptoms of a cold can be greatly helped by simple home treatments. For instance, inhaling the steam off boiling water which has been poured into a pudding bowl and has had menthol crystals (or friar's balsam) dissolved in it, will help clear your chest of phlegm. Paracetamol, or aspirin tablets will relieve headaches, and gargling with soluble aspirin will ease a sore throat.

Antibiotics only help if you have a tendency to get bacterial infections such as bronchitis (see p. 17) after a cold.

CONCUSSION

A hard blow to the head will not only hurt your head, but may bruise your brain. If this happens, you will be knocked out, perhaps only for an instant, and will then feel dizzy and have a headache. This is concussion.

If you are concussed, especially during a game such as football or basketball, it may seem easier to carry on playing than to stop and rest. But it is very important to lie down after being concussed. The headache, and often the sickness, are made worse by not resting. And it can become difficult to distinguish the effects of a bruised brain from the much more serious effects of a ruptured blood vessel in the head.

A ruptured blood vessel can be very dangerous indeed but, luckily, it is very uncommon. However, because of this possibility, anyone who has been knocked out for a long time, or who is clearly not well a few minutes after waking up from a short spell of unconsciousness, should be taken to hospital as soon as possible.

Even if someone appears to have completely recovered, they should not be left alone. If they get a severe headache, become very sick or start to complain of seeing double, they should go to a hospital at once.

If you are knocked out a long way away from a hospital, it is much safer to start going there and risk a wasted journey than wait for possible serious signs to develop.

If you are near a hospital, and have been only mildly concussed, you should lie down quietly, until your headache has gone for twelve hours. This may well mean being off school or work for two or three days. You should not watch television while you have the headache.

CONSTIPATION

Constipation is only a problem if it is causing discomfort or distress. Whether you go the lavatory once a week, or twice a day, is unimportant so long as you are comfortable.

You should not take laxatives regularly without telling a doctor. There are usually simpler ways of sorting out the problem. More fibre in your diet, in the form of green vegetables, fruit and bran-containing cereals and wholemeal bread, will increase the bulk of your motions and increase their frequency. Exercise will help to make your bowel actions more regular.

Upsets related to changes in diet, such as those which occur on holiday, usually settle fairly quickly. For dramatic effect, a bowl of prunes is as good a cure as any!

CONVULSION (see FITS, p. 34)

COUGH (see also CROUP, and WHOOPING COUGH, p. 60)

A cough is the natural way of clearing the throat and the tubes which go into the lungs. If you have an infection, such as a cold, phlegm will collect in the throat and coughing will prevent this phlegm from settling into the lungs and causing a more serious infection.

Although cough mixtures are almost always unnecessary, a cough may be eased with a cough linctus, and the sore throat, which often goes with the cough, may be helped by an aspirin gargle. But, luckily, no medicine will remove a cough which is doing you good.

A nervous cough can be a difficult habit to break because it becomes a useful method of communication. Subconsciously, you may be using it to draw attention to yourself. The best way to get rid of it is to be aware of it; try pinching yourself every time you do it! Try not to let it become a habit you do not notice you have.

CRAMP

Cramps occur when a muscle becomes so tense that it seizes up. Cramps from exercise are unlikely if you are fit, but can happen with violent exertion, especially if you are cold, or have sweated a lot and lost salt. This is particularly likely at the seaside when you are sunbathing and swimming.

Cramps at night are also due to muscle tension. If they are very troublesome, your doctor will be able to help.

CROUP

When very young children get a cold the infection sometimes interferes with their breathing so that they get a harsh, barking cough which is painful and distressing. This is called croup. However, by the age of four or five, almost all children lose the tendency to have croup.

If you are looking after a child who has an attack of croup, keep calm. The cough will only get worse if the child becomes worried or frightened. He or she will breathe and cough more easily if the air is damp, so boil a kettle in the bedroom so that steam fills the air. A doctor should be called in all but the most trivial attacks to give advice and check that all is well.

CUTS

If you cut yourself, do not panic! Most people can lose well over a pint of blood without coming to any harm. Even if the cut is deep, you have lots of time to find a cloth, preferably a clean one, to press against the bleeding point.

Normally, anything except arterial bleeding (see CIRCULATION, p. 20) will dry up within about ten minutes. Dirty wounds should then be cleaned and covered with a sticking plaster. If the cut cannot be easily closed with a plaster, it will need attention from a nurse or doctor and may well need stitching. You should check that you have had an antitetanus injection within the last five years.

CYSTIC FIBROSIS

This is an inherited disease. Sufferers are liable to frequent attacks of bronchitis and pneumonia (see pp. 17 and 44) and may well have to take tablets to aid digestion. In the past, many people died from it when they were very young, but modern methods of treatment mean that the outlook is now very much more hopeful.

This disease is inherited through both parents, and there is a high chance that more than one child in the family will be affected. But if you do not have cystic fibrosis, even if one of your brothers or sisters has it, it is very unlikely that your children will be affected.

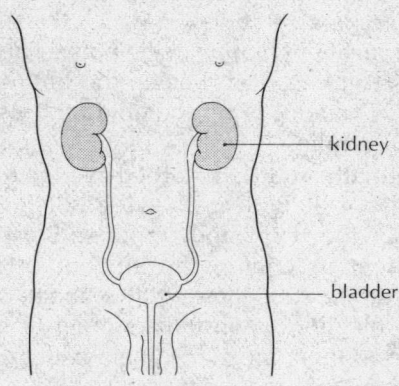

Urine is produced in the kidneys and stored in the bladder until you pass water

CYSTITIS

Cystitis is the name given to an infection of the urine in the bladder. The bacteria which cause cystitis live naturally on the skin, so if you are liable to the infection, it is difficult to prevent. Cystitis is more likely to occur in girls than boys because their urine outlet is closer to their bladder and infection can get in more easily.

The symptoms you will notice are a burning pain when passing water, and a need to go to the lavatory more often than usual. Any other upset to do with passing water may also be caused by cystitis.

If you think you have cystitis, you should go to the doctor. He or she will give you tablets to kill the infection and to clear up the trouble.

Cystitis can be quite unpleasant. You should drink plenty of water to wash the infection through, and, take paracetamol or aspirin to help the pain and fever. Hot baths and gentle washing may relieve some of the discomfort.

DIABETES

Diabetes is a condition in which the sufferer gets too much sugar circulating in the body. This is dangerous, because it can oversweeten the brain and lead to a coma. Diabetes is not curable, and only sometimes runs in families.

Normally, food is absorbed into the body and stored as sugar or fat. Both are then used all through the day as fuel for the brain and muscles. But diabetics need treatment to control the amount of sugar in their bodies. Young people with diabetes almost always need injections of insulin in order to stay healthy. If they miss their injections, the amount of sugar in their bodies may increase dangerously.

Older people can also get diabetes, but they can usually be treated with a special diet or with tablets.

All diabetics have to be careful what they eat. Too much sugary food will sweeten the body dangerously, making them feel ill and pass a lot of water. After a few days they may even fall into a dangerous coma. On the other hand too little nourishment and the daily insulin injection will lower the amount of sugar in the body until there is not enough to feed the muscles and brain. If this happens, they will have what is called a 'hypo'. They will behave very peculiarly for a few minutes and then pass out.

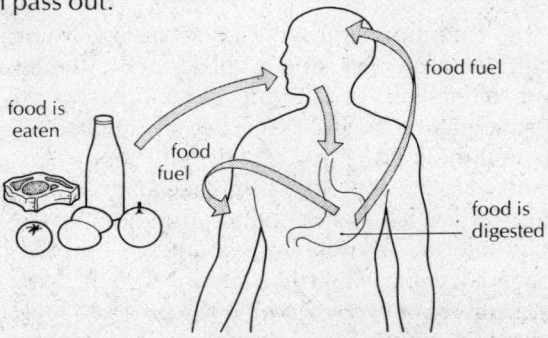

Food fuel is needed to keep your brain and muscles working

So if you have a diabetic friend who starts to behave oddly, give them a sugary drink. They will usually quickly recover. If they are unconscious, get a doctor as soon as possible.

Advice for diabetics

It is very important that you understand what your insulin treatment is doing. The better you control your diabetes, the better it is for you. You should certainly know how to adjust your treatment if you are to have a large meal later than usual, and what to do if you are ill. You should carry a card or wear an identity tag to tell others you are diabetic.

Good control of your diabetes will not only reduce the risk of having a 'hypo' (slipping out of control with too little sugar in your blood and urine); it will also reduce the chance of your developing artery disease (see p. 154) which used to trouble so many middle-aged diabetics. The tendency for diabetics to get artery disease is one reason why it is so important you do not smoke, and why you should have regular check-ups from your doctor.

Do not be afraid to ask a doctor or nurse anything that you want to know. They will always be willing to answer your questions. They realise that diabetes is a complicated condition to understand, and one which has many practical difficulties.

DIARRHOEA

An attack of diarrhoea and sickness may be caused by food poisoning (see FOOD HYGIENE, p. 83) but is more often brought on by an infectious bug. Whatever the cause, the attack is usually over before any drugs that you might take have time to work. It is therefore best to go to bed, drink plenty of water and wait for the attack to pass.

Diarrhoea brought on by excitement or fear is common; you may well have experienced it yourself before an exam. You may get some relief from a simple treatment bought at the chemist.

If diarrhoea occurs every day check with your doctor that all is well. This is especially true if you have noticed blood or mucus in the motions. Some people have loose motions quite normally, but it is best to have a check-up if you are worried.

DISLOCATION

A dislocation occurs when the two bones, which make up a joint, are forced apart. This always damages the joint and is very painful. Rugby players, in particular, may dislocate their shoulders. Once this has happened, there is a tendency for it to occur again. The problem is fairly easily dealt with in a hospital casualty ward, but you should take care in the future. If necessary, a strap can be worn to support the shoulders.

Other joints can be dislocated, and fingers in particular may well be painful for some months after the injury because of the damage to the joint.

Some people have hypermobile joints, sometimes known as 'double' joints. They are useful as a party trick or for amusing your friends, but are otherwise not of importance.

DOWN'S SYNDROME

This condition is also known as mongolism because the distinctive appearance of mongol children reminded early doctors of the eastern oriental race, the Mongols.

Children with Down's syndrome are often mentally retarded. Though lovable, they are often a handful to look after at home, especially as they get older. Yet they are usually very happy children, despite their problems.

Down's syndrome is only very rarely inherited and it would be unusual for two children in a family to suffer from it. But if advice or reassurance is needed, your doctor will be able to tell you what chance there is of an affected child being born into your family.

EAR PROBLEMS

The ear is a very well-designed microphone. Put very simply, sound waves are picked up and channelled down the earhole. The eardrum at the bottom of the earhole then starts the process of converting those waves into nerve messages which tell the brain what sounds we are hearing.

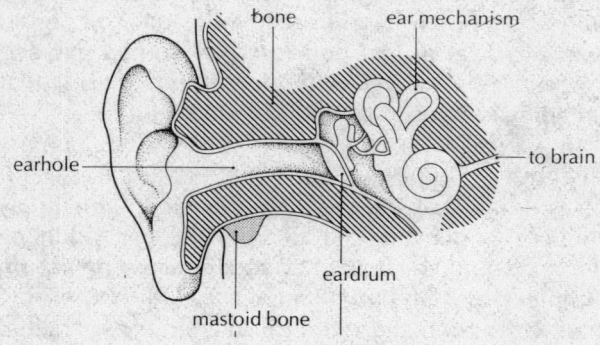

The ear

Deafness

Microphones can break in lots of ways. Similarly, deafness can happen for many different reasons. Temporary deafness caused by a build-up of wax in the ears is the easiest type to solve, but do not poke your eardrums when cleaning your ears, or you will damage them. Also, please try not to drop bits of cotton wool in your ear. Your doctor will not enjoy fishing them out!

Loud noises damage the sensitive mechanisms of the ear. None of us can avoid noise, so older people may often be rather hard of hearing. If the ears are subjected to fairly constant loud noise damage can progress quite quickly and deafness can result. So anyone working in a noisy place, whether they are a factory worker or a pop star, should wear ear muffs.

A series of ear infections will also damage your hearing. An operation may become necessary to minimise the damage the infections are doing.

People who are born deaf are usually deaf for life, although hearing aids can be of considerable help. Some people are deaf because their mothers caught german measles (see p. 37) early on in their pregnancy. For this reason all young girls should be vaccinated against german measles.

Deaf people do not choose to be deaf, and they should be treated with courtesy. If they fail to understand what you say it is probably your fault. You should always look at a deaf person when you speak, and make sure you say everything clearly and slowly so that lipreading is made as easy as possible.

Earache

This is usually caused by an ear infection, which may produce an itchy discharge from the ear. Such an infection should be treated by your doctor, and aspirin or paracetamol tablets will relieve the pain.

Less often, damage to the eardrums causes earache. Particularly sensitive eardrums may be damaged by big air pressure changes. For example, stun-grenades and other explosives immobilise people by bursting their eardrums. Both are used in terrorist attacks, so if you are involved in one, hold your ears!

Small air-pressure changes, such as occur when you dive into a swimming pool, do not usually cause any problems.

Ear operations

These are most often done on young children to repair the damage caused by a series of ear infections, which have blocked up the sensitive parts of the ear.

Adenoids The adenoids are special structures, similar to tonsils (see p. 56), but further back in the throat. When they become enlarged they affect the voice and prevent ear infections from clearing up properly.

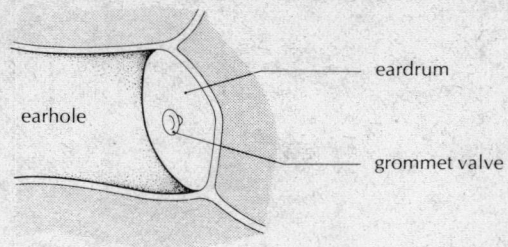

Antral washout The inside of the ear is washed out and cleaned of the debris left by a series of infections.

Grommets Small valves are put into the eardrum. These allow the fluid produced by an infection to drain out of the inner parts of the ear. You will need protection whilst swimming as water can also drain into the ear.

Mastoid The bone just behind the ear is the mastoid bone. It protects the inner parts of the ear. An operation on this bone may be necessary to repair the damaged parts of the ear.

EYE PROBLEMS

The outer layer of the eye, the cornea, is easily damaged by grit or injury. So if any pain or irritation in the eye persists, you should go to a doctor for a check-up. Any delay can cause the trouble to get worse.

Black eye (see BRUISING, p. 17)

Conjunctivitis is the name for a variety of minor infections and inflammations which cause the white of the eye to go red and weepy. These are fairly common, and are best seen by a doctor.

Double vision If you are seeing double, you should tell a doctor. This is particularly true if you have recently banged your head or had a bad headache.

Squint You squint if your two eyes do not look in exactly the same direction. This is fairly common and is

31

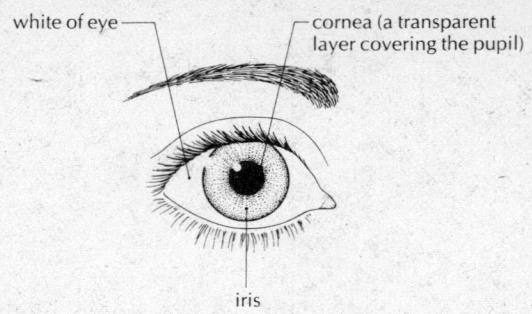

The eye

usually treated before you are five years old. If you still have a squint after this age, one eye, called the master eye, usually does all the seeing. It is then too late for useful treatment. Many people have had operations to cure squints when they were young.

Stye This is a painful infection of the eyelash. It is usually on the upper lid and may occur several times in quick succession. Frequent gentle washing of the eye and the application of a hot compress will usually clear up the trouble.

Glasses and contact lenses

If you need glasses, you will be either astigmatic, short-sighted or long-sighted. All three abnormalities cause your vision to be blurred. Astigmatism is corrected with the help of glasses which compensate for an eyeball which is not quite spherical, while short and long-sightedness is corrected with glasses which assist the eye's natural lens to focus properly. An oculist will make sure you have the correct glasses.

Contact lenses cannot correct long-sightedness and are best for those with mild short-sightedness. However, lenses often cannot be worn all day because they begin to irritate. The newer soft lenses are more fragile, but more comfortable than hard lenses.

Colour blindness
Colour blindness is surprisingly common and affects about one in ten boys and rather fewer girls. You may not notice the defect until you do special tests with coloured cards which show up the problem. Most colour blind people find it difficult to differentiate between red and green. There is no treatment and, unfortunately, colour blindness does bar you from certain types of work. Complete colour blindness is very uncommon.

Other diseases of the eye
There are many diseases which affect the eyes. **Cataracts** are white condensations inside the eye which gradually obscure the sight, usually of old people.

Glaucoma is a disease in which the eyeball's natural tension increases, so that the sight is eventually damaged. Fortunately both these diseases can be treated.

FAINTING

According to popular history, Victorian ladies used to faint at the first hint of romance or danger. Thankfully, girls today have lost this tendency, although both girls and boys do still faint sometimes, especially when they are suffering from heat, emotion and lack of food. This is particularly likely at pop concerts and on parade grounds, but may occur elsewhere.

The faint itself is caused by a lack of blood flowing to the brain. If you lie down, the blood flow is increased and you recover quickly. Although you are more likely to faint if you are not well, fainting itself is not a cause for worry. It is just nature's way of telling you to lie down and rest.

FEVER

If you have a fever your body temperature is several degrees higher than the normal 37°C (98.4°F). A fever is caused by poisons escaping from an infection, or some other disease, into your blood. Certain infections, such as flu (see p. 35), cause quite high temperatures; others have little effect.

Aspirin and paracetamol are both useful in settling a fever. They make you feel better by bringing your temperature down, and by easing aches and pains.

A high fever may cause delirium, which is an unpleasant feeling of confusion and vivid nightmares. In very young children, it can occasionally cause a fit (see below); children under five who are feverish and become very hot should be stripped and sponged down with lukewarm water.

FITS

A fit (or convulsion) is a frightening thing both to experience and to see. It is frightening to experience because it is often unexpected, and when it passes off, it leaves the person feeling sleepy, embarrassed and suffering from a bad headache.

It is frightening to see because the person having the fit goes stiff, and then starts to shake uncontrollably for a minute or so. It is impossible to wake them, and you may think they are dying. Try to keep calm, and lie the person on their side so that if they are sick the vomit will flow out of their mouth and not choke them. Loosen any tight clothing so that they can breathe easily.

Epilepsy

Most people with epilepsy are normal individuals who are unlucky enough to have occasional fits. They are not ill or diseased, and the epilepsy often decreases as the years go by. Once they have started taking special tablets some epileptics never have another fit. Others continue to have regular attacks.

Some children have a type of epilepsy called **petit mal**. With this, the child simply becomes dreamy and unreachable for a few seconds. Very young children may have fits with a high temperature (see FEVER, p. 33).

Fits can also be caused by other conditions which may or may not lead to mental handicap (see p. 109). Anybody with simple epilepsy will have had tests to show that it is not caused by one of these conditions.

FLU

Flu is short for influenza and is caused by the influenza virus. There are several different types of flu, and this is why vaccination against it is not always effective. You may well get vaccinated against the wrong type of flu!

Flu is worse than a cold, although the treatment is the same (see p. 21). It is sensible to take several days off school or work, since the illness is very infectious and will leave you feeling weak and drained.

FRACTURE

A fracture is the medical word for any break, crack or chip in a bone. A cracked bone is painful, but not usually very serious. If it is to heal properly, the two halves of the bone have to be kept in alignment, so you should avoid doing anything which may hurt the injured area.

Cracked skulls and cracked ribs usually heal themselves with little or no treatment, while a crack in a wrist or collar bone, for example, needs only supportive bandaging or a sling.

'Green-stick' fractures

A young person's wrist bone will often not break right through, but will bend and crack like a green branch or twig. The doctor may call it a 'green-stick' fracture, and again it usually needs only a period of support in plaster for it to heal.

Sometimes, however, the wrist bone is bent so much that it needs to be straightened before the plaster is put

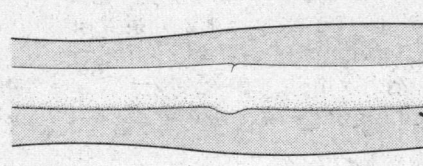

A greenstick fracture

on. This usually requires an operation under anaesthetic.

More serious fractures

If you break a leg or elbow bone, the break is usually a clean one. In this case the bone must be fixed in plaster if it is to heal properly. If it is badly broken, it may be necessary to have an operation to straighten the bone. Metal screws are sometimes inserted to hold the broken ends of bone in place.

If you are in hospital with a broken leg, try not to make yourself more unfit by eating and smoking too much. Doing this will slow down your recovery.

A broken back or broken neck may or may not damage the spinal cord. (The spinal cord is the cord of nerves which runs from the brain down the backbone

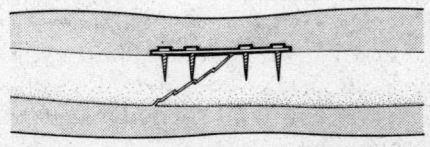

A bone after a pin and plate operation

to the rest of the body.) If this cord is damaged, you may be paralysed below the level of the injury; if it is not damaged, you will probably recover completely.

If you find a badly injured person after an accident, it is best not to move them. If you have to move them, take great care to keep their back straight.

GERMAN MEASLES (RUBELLA)

German measles is a very minor illness which you can get without even noticing it. It is unusual to get the disease twice.

German measles only becomes important if a woman catches it in the first few months of pregnancy when her tiny developing baby may also catch the disease. Five or six months later it may be born with incurable deafness or a bad heart problem. German measles in pregnancy is not always harmful, especially in the later months, but all schoolgirls should be vaccinated against it. Refusing this vaccination is to risk having a damaged baby.

GLANDULAR FEVER

Despite being popularly known as 'the kissing disease', glandular fever is spread in a similar way to a cold. Obviously if you kiss somebody with a cold, you are likely to get a cold too, but just being in the same room with them can also give it to you.

Many people have had glandular fever without knowing it. Only if you get it badly is a doctor likely to do the necessary tests to prove that you have it. Usually you will just have a sore throat and swollen glands, which could be caused by any flu-like cold.

However, a bad attack of glandular fever can be quite unpleasant and make you feel ill and miserable for up to several months. There is no cure, so it is simply a matter of waiting for the attack to pass off. The only consolation is that you will not get it twice.

HAY FEVER

This is an unpleasant condition which is usually worst during the spring and summer. It makes you feel ill, and when there are certain grass pollens in the air, it makes you sneeze and gives you sore, runny eyes. This is because you are allergic to these pollens (see ALLERGY, p. 9).

Hay fever can be eased by antihistamine tablets from a doctor, but these may make you sleepy. If the hay fever causes a lot of trouble, you may be given a course of injections from your doctor to help ease the symptoms. The only cure is to avoid the pollen completely . . . holidays in the Arctic might be the answer!

HEADACHE (see also CONCUSSION, p. 21)

Headaches have a variety of causes. Very severe, throbbing headaches, which occur again and again, and which affect your vision, are probably due to **migraine** (see p. 46), but if you have a bad headache which makes you feel ill, or if you have regular headaches which are not eased with aspirin or paracetamol tablets, it would be sensible to consult your doctor.

Tension headaches

Many people think they suffer from migraines when, in fact, they are suffering from tension headaches. These are very common, and are brought on by tiredness or overwork. Your brain is trying to say 'I want to rest', and not surprisingly the headache goes away if you take it easy for a time.

Other types of headache

Girls may find they get headaches when they have their period. These are due to natural hormonal activity, but if they are very bad, your doctor may be able to help with advice or treatment.

Headaches are not often caused by eye-strain, but if you have not had your eyes tested recently, it would be a good idea to have them checked.

HERNIA

A hernia is a bulge in the abdominal wall caused by pressure from the intestines. The bulge is usually small, but however big it is there is no chance of the intestines bursting through the wall. It may be uncomfortable, but is usually just a bit tiresome.

Since a hernia increases in size, even if quite slowly, an operation is done to strengthen the weakness in the abdominal wall, which is usually in the groin area or around the navel. This operation means staying in hospital for about a week, and avoiding heavy lifting for three months after that.

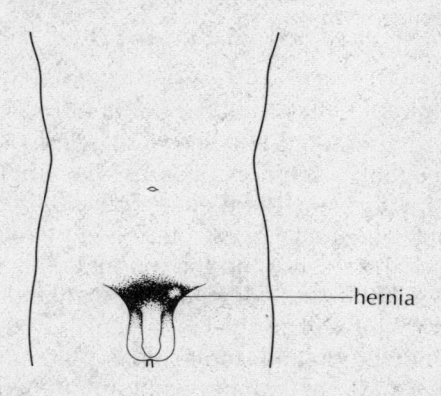

One of the places where a hernia can occur

INDIGESTION

Mild indigestion, or heartburn, is a common ailment and usually disappears quite quickly of its own accord.

Eating large meals at irregular intervals is likely to upset your digestion. Like you, your stomach prefers a little work at predictable intervals to huge amounts

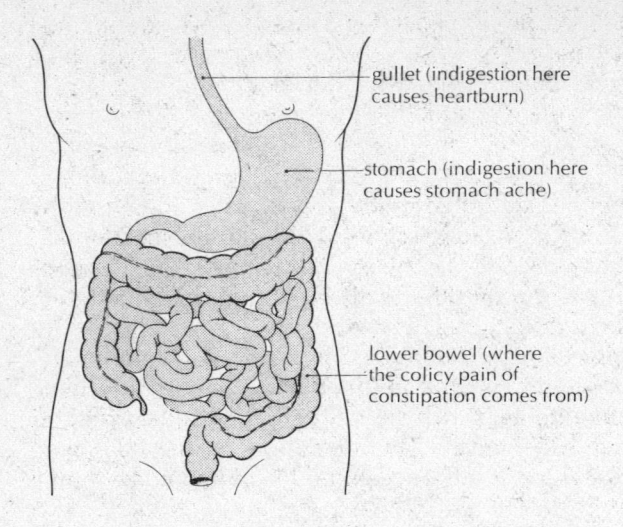

- gullet (indigestion here causes heartburn)
- stomach (indigestion here causes stomach ache)
- lower bowel (where the colicy pain of constipation comes from)

Pain in your abdomen

arriving unexpectedly! To avoid both indigestion and constipation, try to eat a balanced diet (see p. 80).

If you find that indigestion mixtures from the chemist are helpful, it is likely that you are developing some irritation in your stomach from the food that you are eating. Avoiding alcohol and spicy foods helps prevent it and milky drinks, including tea, soothe the discomfort. Not smoking will also help.

Severe indigestion and stomach pains are different. Your doctor may feel that the symptoms are worrying enough to justify blood tests and X-rays (see p. 180). If these show up an ulcer (see p. 168) or gall-bladder trouble, the problem can be treated.

It is more difficult when there is no obvious problem which needs treatment. Some unlucky people have a lot of stomach pain for which no cause is ever found. In a few cases this is brought on by worry or overwork, but in others this is not so. Do not think that an operation is necessarily the answer.

INFECTION (see also FOOD HYGIENE, p. 83)

There are many different types of infection. Most of the common infections are caused either by bacteria germs or virus germs. All infections are to some extent catching.

Bacterial infections

Infections caused by bacteria usually improve if left untreated, but may need antibiotic treatment (see p. 95) from a doctor if the infection starts to spread. Common infections caused by bacteria include ear infections, pneumonia and the infections that affect cuts or grazes.

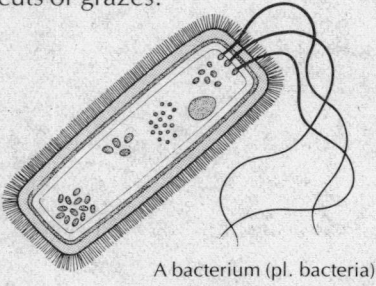

A bacterium (pl. bacteria)
Bacteria move around and multiply easily to spread disease

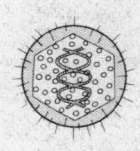

A virus
Viruses are very small and can only grow inside the body

Viral infections

Infections caused by viruses are often easy to catch, but they almost always get better of their own accord. They include the common cold, flu, mild stomach upsets and childhood diseases like measles and mumps. Antibiotics have no effect against viruses.

Other types of infection

Rarer types of infection may be caused by a variety of other types of germ. For instance, athlete's foot is caused by a fungus which grows on the skin; threadworms are caused by minute worms that live in the lower part of the intestines.

JAUNDICE

Jaundice is easily recognised by yellowing of the skin and the whites of the eyes. This means that the liver is not working as well as it should. Normally, the yellow chemicals are absorbed by the liver, but if you have jaundice they are taken up by the skin instead and they stain it yellow.

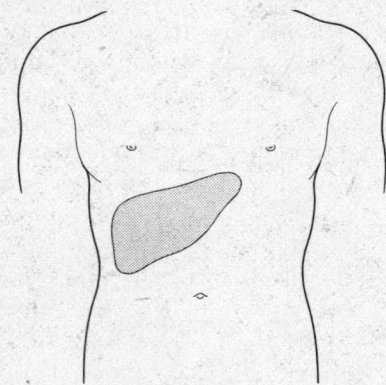

Your liver is situated under your ribs on your right side

Hepatitis
Jaundice is usually caused by an infection of the liver called hepatitis. This disease makes you feel quite ill, but almost always gets better of its own accord. You should not drink alcohol while you have the disease because it can strain the weakened liver.

Yellow fever
Yellow fever is a nasty infection which you can catch in Central and South American countries and in Central Africa. It is called this because it gives you jaundice. You should be vaccinated against it if the health regulations of the country you are to visit require you to do so.

Other types of jaundice
Someone with a weak liver may get jaundice just by drinking heavily. Gall bladder trouble can also lead to

jaundice, but this type usually gets better rather more quickly.

LARYNGITIS

Laryngitis is an infection very similar to a cold. With a cold, the nose and throat are mainly affected, but with laryngitis, the voice box is the focus of the trouble.

If you have any difficulty in breathing you should see a doctor. Usually, however, you will only notice that you are hoarse and feel under the weather. Go to bed, stop talking and wait to feel better! Aspirin, taken either as a tablet dissolved in water or as a gargle, will relieve some of the discomfort; and boiling a kettle in the room to moisten the air may also help. Antibiotics are unlikely to help as the infection is usually caused by a virus (see INFECTION, p. 41).

LUNGS

Apart from your heart (which is about the size of a grapefruit), all the space inside your ribs is taken up by your lungs. You can feel the position of your heart if you put one finger between your ribs just below the left nipple and press gently. Your finger will move slightly with the beating of your heart.

With each beat of the heart, blood is pumped round the body and through the lungs. Now take a deep breath. Air rushes into your mouth and nose and down into your lungs. The jet of air passes down your windpipe, the middle part of which you can feel at the front of your neck. The lower part of the windpipe is in the chest where it divides into two tubes, one of which leads to the left lung and one to the right.

These two tubes are called bronchi, and an infection in the bronchi causes the cough of bronchitis. An infection in the windpipe causes a sore throat, and may lead to tonsilitis (see p. 56) or laryngitis (see above).

The lung itself is like an air-filled sponge. Air is

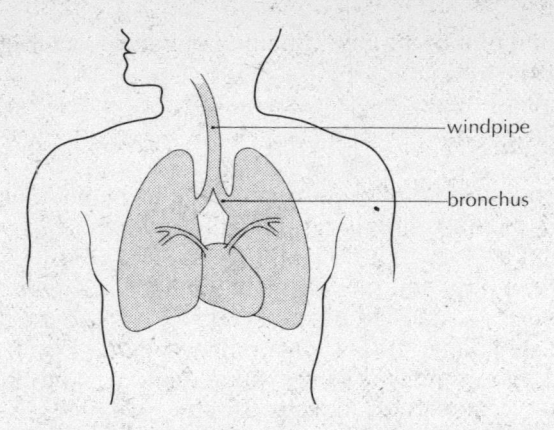

Your heart and lungs are situated in your chest under your ribs

squeezed in and out of the lungs by way of the bronchi and windpipe. In the lungs, oxygen is absorbed from the air and then passed into the blood which is circulating through the lung tissue. Without oxygen, you would die. The complicated chemistry which keeps your muscles working and your brain thinking needs oxygen as its fuel.

When you breathe out, air is pushed out of the lungs to make room for a fresh supply. Meanwhile, even though you do not notice it, your heart keeps on beating – pumping your blood round the body.

Pneumonia

Infection in the lungs is called pneumonia. This makes you feel quite ill and causes a cough and shortness of breath. It is not painful unless the infection reaches the lining of the lung and causes **pleurisy**. Pleurisy makes it hurt to breathe. This is because of the sore areas on the outer lining of the lung which, fortunately, usually heal fairly quickly.

Pneumonia can be quite a serious disease in babies and in old people. It usually heals fairly quickly with antibiotic tablets from a doctor, but sometimes hospital treatment is necessary.

If the outside lining of the lung leaks, air can escape from the lung and collect under the ribs. This is called a **pneumothorax**. It can be dangerous, because the air fills the chest and forces the lung to collapse. Very occasionally, this suddenly happens to a healthy person, and although it is easily dealt with in hospital, it can be a frightening experience.

MEASLES

The most obvious symptom of measles is a blotchy rash. But it can also cause a fever (see p. 33) with a runny nose and sore eyes.

Because measles can occasionally lead to more serious conditions, like pneumonia (see LUNGS, p. 43), young children should be vaccinated against it.

A person with measles is infectious for several days before the rash appears, and for a week thereafter.

MENINGITIS

There are two types of this fairly common illness. Both are caused by an infection of the lining of the brain (not of the brain itself) which results in a nasty headache and a stiff painful neck.

Viral meningitis

The more usual type of meningitis, caused by a virus infection (see p. 41), is seldom dangerous and antibiotic treatment is not needed. You only need to take aspirin or paracetamol to control the severe headache.

Bacterial meningitis

Bacterial meningitis is a serious illness. Nowadays, antibiotic treatment is almost always successful and the infection quickly clears up, but a persistent infection can cause noticeable after-effects. If you have had meningitis and are not aware of any after-effects, you have made a complete recovery.

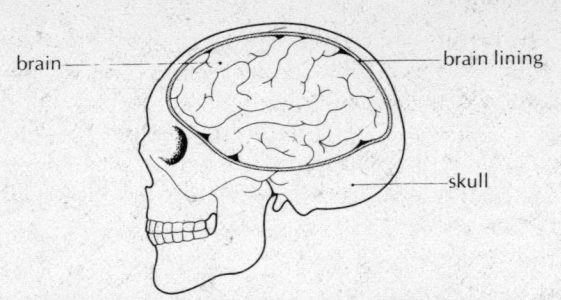

The lining of your brain is damaged in an attack of meningitis. The brain itself is not usually affected

If your doctor suspects that you might have meningitis, he will send you to a hospital for a lumbar puncture. This is not a particularly pleasant experience as it involves taking a sample of fluid from inside the spine with a needle and syringe. However, the few uncomfortable, rather than painful, minutes are worth going through to ensure that you get the treatment that you need.

MIGRAINE (see also HEADACHE, p. 38)

Migraine is a condition where severe, throbbing headaches occur again and again. Many people have mild headaches which may or may not be due to migraine, but migraine itself is effectively treated with special tablets. A severe attack of migraine is very unpleasant and it is essential to lie down in a dark room to minimise the discomfort.

MUMPS

This is a common illness which you may catch about two and a half weeks after seeing somebody with mumps. You can only get it once.

Mumps mainly attack the salivary glands, making it difficult to swallow. It also affects the sex organs. But it would need a bad attack of mumps, causing pain in both testicles or ovaries, to give even a slight risk of sterility. Your doctor will be able to reassure you, if you are worried.

MUSCULAR DYSTROPHY

Muscular dystrophy is a disease of the muscles. It tends to run in families and there are several different types.

A child who has muscular dystrophy grows up with his or her muscles becoming progressively weaker. Yet although the disease is incurable, much can be done to help the child cope with his or her difficulties. However, those most seriously affected — boys with **duchenne muscular dystrophy** — grow up to be confined to a wheelchair.

NOSE

A nose is a brilliant piece of design. It warms the air that you breathe in and it cools the air that you breathe out. This cooling effect, especially in winter, causes water to condense, and means that in very cold weather you will always have a drip on the end of your nose.

Blocked nose

This is one of the least enjoyable features of a bad cold. Most chemists sell effective decongestants which unblock the nose. Otherwise inhaling the steam of cooling boiled water in which menthol crystals have been dissolved, is an old-fashioned remedy which works very well. Vick, or a similar vapour rub is also useful.

If one nostril is blocked most of the time, it is possible that the septum (the wall between the two nostrils) is out of place. But whatever the cause of the blockage, it is rarely troublesome enough to justify an operation.

Broken nose

After a thump on the nose, the nose swells up very swiftly, especially if a bone is broken. If a bone is merely cracked, it will heal up well. But even if it has been forced out of place, no treatment is usually possible until the bruising has gone down. If necessary, the bone can then be reset in hospital.

If, soon after the injury, you notice that the septum (see above) is swollen and painful, you should see a doctor. A large bruise in the septum may cause damage to the nasal bones.

Cosmetic surgery

All noses have character, but you may not like your nose or feel that it does not suit your face. Confidence in your own appearance is important, and it is all too easy to allow an unkind remark to dent it. But even if this happens, do try to remember real friends are more interested in you as a person than in the shape or size of your nose.

Having said this, if you really feel you cannot live with your nose, it is possible to have it altered. But your doctor will need a lot of persuading before he or she will let you have an expensive and painful operation which, like all operations, carries a slight risk.

Nosebleeds (see BLEEDING, p. 16)

Rhinitis

This occurs when the lining of the nose becomes inflamed because of an allergy (see p. 9). It is often difficult to find out what is causing the trouble, but the persistent soreness and runny nose may be helped by a spray from a doctor.

PERITONITIS

The intestines are normally coiled up neatly inside the abdomen. Food moves slowly through them, from mouth to anus, and is digested over a period of about two days.

But if the intestines become blocked, or if they burst,

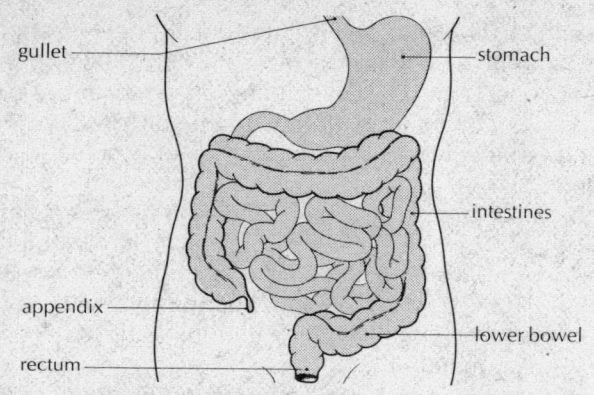

The intestines are covered with a special lining. This becomes damaged during an attack of peritonitis

a very dangerous condition develops, which almost always leads to peritonitis. Peritonitis is a severe infection which poisons and paralyses the intestines, and makes the sufferer very ill quite quickly. A burst appendix is one cause of this condition.

The only safe way to treat peritonitis is to have an operation to wash away the infection from inside the abdomen. It always takes some weeks to recover from the illness and its treatment, and you can expect to be off school or work for at least two months.

PREGNANCY (see p. 137)

SHOCK

Newspaper reports of accidents often say that someone has been 'taken to hospital suffering from shock'. This is another way of saying that though they were not injured, they needed to go to hospital for a check-up. After any accident, the victim, especially if he or she is old, needs a few hours to come to terms with what has happened.

Most accident victims are dazed and confused at first, but it often happens that they need a quiet cup of tea much more than an upsetting ride in an ambulance. So, if you are on the scene of an accident, check to see if anyone is hurt before calling an ambulance. But remember that anyone who has been unconscious, or who is bleeding, or in pain will need hospital treatment.

To a doctor, shock means something completely different. If a patient is 'in shock', he is very badly injured or ill, and needs immediate emergency treatment. The patient is cold, clammy and weak, but should not be given anything to drink as he may need an urgent operation.

SICKNESS (VOMITING)

Being sick is unpleasant, but it serves a useful purpose by getting rid of food that might do you harm. If you have eaten or drunk too much, you may well be sick and it is unfair to blame the sickness on food poisoning! But whatever the cause, there is no treatment that will help this sort of sickness. You just have to wait for the poisons to work their way out of your system.

Vomiting combined with other symptoms such as a bad headache, severe stomach pains or pain on passing water, could possibly indicate something more serious and you should see your doctor.

Morning sickness

Morning sickness is one of the first signs of pregnancy (see p. 137). Therefore, any girl who starts feeling nauseous, or is actually sick, in the mornings should have a pregnancy test as soon as possible.

Travel sickness

Motion, or travel, sickness is very common. Considerable relief can be obtained from travel pills, available at most chemists.

SINUSITIS

Sinusitis is an infection in the sinuses which results in a stuffed-up feeling and a drippy nose.

The sinuses are hollow spaces in the bones of the cheeks and forehead. They are like caves in the bones of the face which open through tiny tunnels into the inside of the nose. If you have sinusitis, your doctor will probably give you antibiotics to clear it up. But it is not a common illness and a cold will often give much the same symptoms.

If you get sinusitis often, your doctor may advise you to have an operation to wash the sinuses out. Hopefully, this will clear up the trouble once and for all.

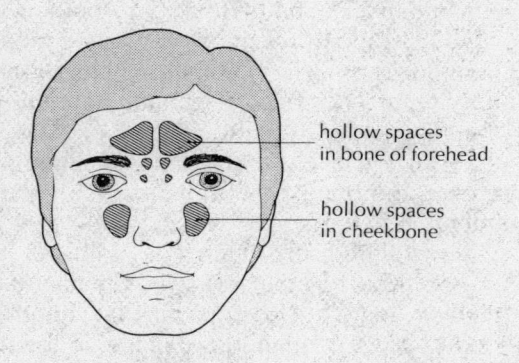

hollow spaces in bone of forehead

hollow spaces in cheekbone

The position of the sinuses

SORE THROAT

A sore throat is usually caused by a viral infection (see p. 41); it is one of the features of a cold. Antibiotics are not useful for this type of infection, but may help bad sore throats caused by bacterial infections.

Since it is unwise to take any tablets unnecessarily, you should only go to a doctor with a sore throat when it is really bad and has lasted longer than usual. Aspirin gargles will relieve the discomfort of most sore throats.

SPRAIN

A sprain can be extremely painful, and may lead you to think you have broken the limb you have in fact sprained. But try to be brave! It is very embarrassing to be carried into a hospital casualty department screaming that your leg is broken, and then hobble out an hour later with a bandage round your sprainèd ankle.

A sprain is caused by an unexpected pull on a joint — usually the ankle or knee — and this pull stretches, and so bruises one of the many muscles or ligaments which move and support the joint. If one of the muscles or ligaments is also torn, the sprain will take that much longer to get better.

Most sprains can be treated by binding the joint to support it, and by resting as much as possible. Use your common sense when deciding whether or not to go to a busy emergency department at a hospital. Remember that if you have a sprain, you will probably not notice the pain until a few minutes after the injury; if you have broken the bone, the pain is usually immediate and intense.

Any sprain will stretch the ligaments holding the bones close together. These ligaments take time to recover, so try not to sprain the same joint again as this may cause a permanent weakness in the joint. If you have a weak ankle, it helps to wear a bandage support when you take exercise.

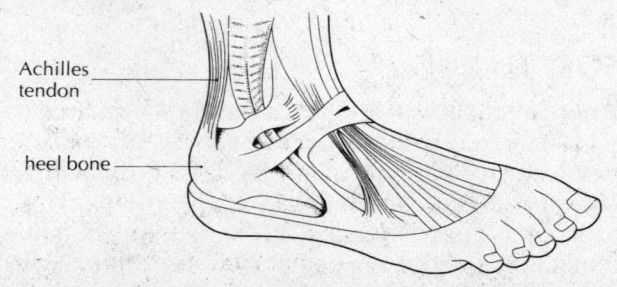

If any ligament in this complicated system is damaged, you will have a painful sprain

Sprained knees can be more troublesome because there is cartilage in the joint which, though it provides stability to the knee, is liable to damage in an accident. This can take rather longer to clear up, and if injured more than once, may keep on giving trouble. Occasionally an operation is needed to help, though it does not usually completely cure, the problem.

STAMMER

A stammer occurs when your mind works faster than you can say what you are thinking. Many very young children stammer when they are learning to speak, but they usually grow out of it.

If a stammer persists, or appears when you are nervous, it may become tiresome enough to justify going to a speech therapist. He or she will train you to speak each word clearly, and this helps to control the stammer. Stammers almost always lessen as you get older.

STOMACH ACHE

When someone has a bad stomach ache they often think they have appendicitis (see p. 11). But appendicitis is much more serious than an ordinary stomach ache, and makes you feel very ill, not just uncomfortable. Most stomach aches are caused by indigestion (see p. 39).

Many stomach pains are caused by some form of spasm in the bowel. This may be caused by constipation or, possibly, by overeating. If this sort of pain – a colicy pain which comes and goes – often troubles you, try following the advice given under CONSTIPATION (see p. 22) on healthy, regular diets.

Children often get stomach pains when they have a cold or other mild infection. Just as glands in the neck may swell up, so similar glands in the stomach may also swell a little and cause pain.

A urine infection (see CYSTITIS, p. 24) or kidney infection can cause stomach pains.

Sometimes there is no obvious physical reason for the pain. In this case, there may be no particular cause (see INDIGESTION, p. 40).

TEETH

It is plain commonsense to look after your teeth. The better you treat them when you are young, the less trouble they will give you later on. If you never washed the plates off which you ate, they would soon be filthy with food stains. The acid produced by the rotting food would eat into them, and within a few months they would start to crumble away.

Your teeth are the same. They need frequent washing, and if they are to last sixty years or more, they also need regular repairs. So make sure you brush your teeth twice a day — ideally after breakfast and just before you go to bed — and visit the dentist every six months. This applies whether you are one of those lucky people with very good teeth, or if your teeth always seem to have holes in them, however well you look after them.

Plaque

Foods which are sweet and sticky encourage the growth of acid-producing bugs which attack teeth. These bugs grow in plaque, a white film which you can see on your own teeth if you scrape the top of them with a fingernail. You can also buy plaque revealing tablets which stain teeth red wherever there is plaque. You then remove the stain, and the plaque, by brushing.

Vigorous brushing of the teeth and a diet high in fibre will keep plaque away and so protect the teeth. Dental floss also helps remove plaque and food between the teeth (it is a type of plastic string, which can be bought at most chemists).

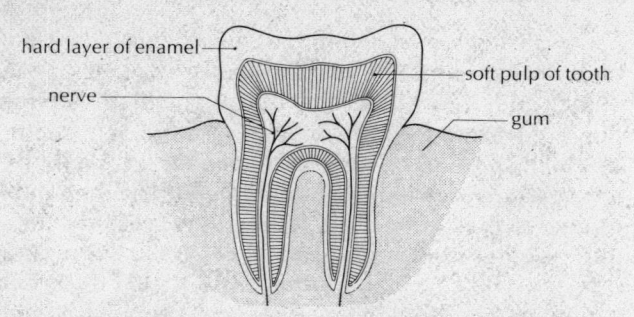

Plaque spreads over the enamel of the tooth and corrodes it

Fluoride

There is no doubt at all that fluoride prevents holes forming in your teeth by making the tooth enamel harder. Even if you live in an area where fluoride is added to the water, it is a good idea to use toothpaste which contains fluoride, particularly if your teeth are still growing (your last wisdom tooth will appear when you are about twenty-two).

Toothache

Toothache is almost always caused by an infection in a damaged tooth. If one of your teeth hurts, go to your dentist, even if the pain goes away. The damage will not get better of its own accord. Aspirin or codeine tablets will take the edge off the pain.

If you are really in pain with your toothache, it might be worth trying a traditional Chinese method of pain relief until you get to the dentist. Take two cubes of ice and wrap them in a thin cloth. Then fold the cloth so that one cube rests either side of the web of skin between your finger and thumb. Do it to the hand that is on the same side of the toothache. It really does work!

TIREDNESS

You do not always feel tired simply because you need sleep — although this is obviously the most usual cause.

Dissatisfaction with your life can also make you feel tired. In this case, you may feel run-down, lacking in energy and even a bit tearful. But although this feeling may sometimes go on for a week or more, it is important to try and stay cheerful. If you let the feeling get on top of you, you will find yourself becoming more and more depressed. Remember that however bad everything seems at the time, sooner or later, you will almost certainly find a new friend or enthusiasm to lift you out of your rut.

Feeling tired for a few days after an attack of flu or a bad cold is quite common. And it takes some weeks to get over an operation under anaesthetic. Anaemia (see p. 11) can also give this feeling of exhaustion. If there is no obvious cause for your tiredness, you should go to a doctor for a check-up.

TONSILITIS

The tonsils are situated on either side of the throat at the back of the mouth. There are two of them and they are large and easy to see in children, but almost invisible in adults.

You have tonsils to prevent infections, which cause sore throats, from spreading to the rest of the body. So if you get tonsilitis, they are only doing their job — although rather too well! An attack of tonsilitis may clear up more quickly if treated with antibiotics.

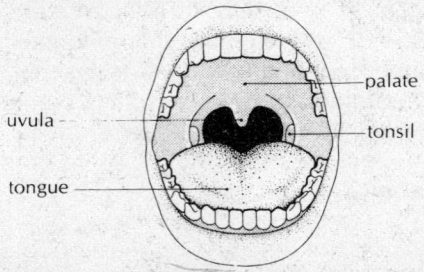

If you open your mouth and look into a mirror, this is what you will see

Tonsils only need to be removed if they become so damaged by frequent attacks of tonsilitis that they do more harm than good. Having them taken out will not affect how often you get a cold.

Since your tonsils become worn-out and shrivelled by the time you reach your late teens, it is often better to put up with attacks of tonsilitis than go through with an operation.

TROPICAL DISEASES

Tropical diseases are infections that spread easily in hot countries. Most only affect those who live where these diseases are common, and who do not take precautions against them. Tourists are usually only at risk if they live rough. An exception to this rule is a chest infection called **legionnaires disease**. This is an illness which may occur in a hotel whose water supply is contaminated. It can happen in even the best hotel, although this is less likely now that it is possible to check for the bug which causes it.

Leprosy
Leprosy is common all over the poorer parts of the world, but a tourist is very unlikely to catch it. It is a skin disease, which leads to deformity.

Malaria
Malaria is a nasty infection of the blood spread by mosquitoes. It is easy to avoid catching this disease by taking special tablets, either daily or weekly (depending on the brand), which will prevent the disease developing. A doctor or travel agent will advise you which countries you need protection in, and for how long the tablets should be taken.

Smallpox
Smallpox no longer causes disease in the world. It has been wiped out by a world-wide campaign of vaccina-

tion in one of the few really magnificent examples of international co-operation. Sadly the germ is still stored in a few laboratories, ready to escape and re-start the disease.

Typhoid and cholera
Typhoid and cholera both cause severe diarrhoea (see p. 27), and vaccination is wise if you intend to travel off the beaten track in any part of the world. They are both dangerous illnesses.

Yellow fever
Yellow fever, a disease prevalent in Central and South America and Central Africa, is a nasty blood infection which is spread by mosquitoes and causes jaundice (see p. 42). You should be vaccinated if you are going near the risk area.

TUBERCULOSIS
Tuberculosis, sometimes known as TB, is a nasty illness which usually affects the lungs and causes a bad cough. It is now treatable, but it used to be a frightening killer disease. In those days it was called consumption.

Tuberculosis is still a problem in some parts of the world, although it has been fairly well controlled by vaccination. Nowadays, at around the age of thirteen, many school children are offered a Heaf test, a scratch on the arm that tells the doctor or nurse whether you are liable to catch TB. If you are, you will be vaccinated with a BCG injection, and will then be protected against it.

VEINS (see also CIRCULATION, p. 20)
Veins are the blood vessels which carry blood from the parts of the body where it has been used back to the heart. If you hang your arm over the side of a chair, you will see your veins clearly on your arm and hand.

Varicose veins
Varicose veins on the legs are veins which have become swollen because the blood is flowing too slowly. They can be itchy and may look rather unsightly. They are helped by wearing firm socks or stockings, but can only be removed by an operation in hospital.

VOMITING (see SICKNESS, p. 50)

WHEEZING
Old people become wheezy with bronchitis (see p. 17) or heart trouble (see p. 163), and young children become wheezy if they have a cold. Older children and adults who wheeze almost always have asthma.

Asthma
Asthma is caused by an allergic reaction in the smallest airway tubes in the lungs (p. 43). This allergic reaction partially blocks the tubes, so that it becomes more difficult to breathe. You start wheezing.

If you have asthma, you have probably already noticed that you wheeze more when you have a cold or if you are in a dusty atmosphere. Many asthmatics also wheeze more after they have been running around or if they are upset.

Sometimes it may help to go to a hospital, and find out what brings on the wheezing attacks. Some people are allergic to one particular thing (see ALLERGY, p. 9), which brings on their asthma, and this can be confirmed with special tests.

Anybody who gets wheezing attacks should see a doctor. Treatment, usually in the form of aerosol inhalers, is very effective, and often makes you feel better than you expected – because you had never realised how much your wheezing was slowing you down. If you get frequent attacks, daily treatment (usually with an inhaler) will often help to reduce their number.

WHOOPING COUGH

You can only get whooping cough once, but it can be a serious illness, especially in babies. So, unless there is any special reason why vaccination is unwise (and a doctor can tell you about this), all babies should be vaccinated against it.

There has been some argument about the possibility of brain damage caused by the whooping cough vaccine, but it is still safer to have the injection than the illness. If you are in doubt, discuss the problem with a health visitor or doctor.

Somebody with whooping cough is infectious for about three weeks after the cough starts. The illness often lasts for up to three months.

WORMS

The thought of having worms is not a pleasant one, but it is a fact that getting rid of worms is almost always very easy, and they rarely do any harm.

Threadworms are a fairly common cause of itching around the anus, especially at night. A doctor will be able to confirm the infection, and give you tablets to deal with the trouble. Threadworms are completely harmless.

2
Skin Problems

You are probably very aware of your appearance – and rightly so. If you are sure you look your best, you will almost certainly find it easier to get on with other people. But try not to worry too much about your looks. Spots and other blemishes come and go. It is worth remembering that they are usually much more visible close up in a mirror than they are across a room. They are certainly less important than you think.

Remember that your skin reflects your state of health. A well-trained racehorse looks frisky and glossy. A well-kept greyhound glows with health. If you have no exercise, no sleep and unhealthy habits, do not be surprised if your skin looks pasty and mottled and you have lank, greasy hair.

Get into training, eat sensibly and keep control of your social life – and you will look and feel far better.

ACNE

Spots are the curse of the teenager. They always seem to be at their worst at the very time it is most important to look good! And it is small consolation to be told that other people are unlikely to notice your spots.

Acne is commonly caused by the skin changes which occur at puberty. The skin generally becomes greasier, and little pockets of infection are trapped by this grease and produce spots. The trouble occurs particularly where small hairs collect the grease and act as a focus for the infection. The main places affected are the face, the neck and the back.

Keeping your skin clean

Simple measures are often of considerable help. Cleanliness is very important. You should wash at least once a day, preferably all over. Use only a mild soap, as a stronger one will dry out the skin and weaken it, making the trouble worse. Some soaps have an antiseptic added to them, and these can be useful. They should not be used more often than is suggested on the packet.

If your skin is very greasy, it will help to wash all the affected areas up to four times every day. But do remember that violent scrubbing of the skin, and the use of over-strong soaps, will do more harm than good. The skin will be damaged and liable to infection.

Girls who wear make-up should be especially careful to clean their faces thoroughly before going to sleep at night.

It is no good washing the skin, and then covering it with a dirty shirt, or allowing dirty hair to fall over it. So if your back or neck is spotty, change your vest or bra every day and your shirt or blouse at least every other day.

Keeping your hair clean

It also helps to keep dandruff and greasy hair under control. If your scalp is unhealthy, with lots of dandruff or heavy grease, it is likely that the skin on your face and neck is not as healthy as it could be. Experiment with shampoos, until you find one that suits you. A medicated shampoo may help, but try simple shampoos first. Most people wash their hair about once every three days, but you may need to wash yours more often. A few people need to wash theirs daily.

Spots on the forehead are made worse by hair falling on to them, especially if it is greasy. Despite the embarrassment, it is better to sweep your hair back instead of trying to hide the spots behind your fringe.

Another reason for keeping your hair off your forehead is to allow sunlight to fall on the spots. Sunlight helps to clear up spots because the ultraviolet light in the rays of the sun has an antiseptic effect. As a result, many people notice that their spots improve during the summer, especially if they have got a tan. So try not to be put off sunbathing because you are embarrassed about your spots. It really does help.

Dogs and horses lose their coats' normal healthy sheen if they are ill, upset or short of exercise. Humans are the same: they need to be fit, have plenty of sleep and not too many emotional problems if they are to look their best. So do not be surprised if tiredness or anxiety brings on a rash of spots.

You may notice that the severity of your acne is affected by what you eat. Chocolate and cheese occasionally make acne worse, as do greasy and fatty foods. But people do differ, so watch out to see if any foods make your condition worse.

All these measures will help to control your acne, but they will not clear it up altogether. Generally speaking, the milder the acne the quicker it is likely to disappear. Severe acne will improve greatly over a few years, but can go on giving occasional trouble for quite some time.

Severe acne can be helped by treatment from a doctor, though there is no point in getting special tablets or lotions unless you follow the advice given above. Before spending a lot of money on acne cures, get advice from your doctor about which creams are likely to help your skin.

ATHLETE'S FOOT

This condition, which is irritating rather than serious, is caused by a fungus which feeds on damp skin. It affects the soles of the feet, and the spaces between the toes, and can be painfully itchy.

Athlete's foot usually clears up fairly quickly if you wash your feet two or three times a day, dry them thoroughly each time and then dust them with talcum powder. You should change your socks or tights every day, and wear shoes that allow air to circulate and cool your feet. Occasionally, medicated talc or cream from a chemist may be necessary.

Athlete's foot is mildly infectious, so if you have got it do not borrow other people's socks or tights or walk around in bare feet.

BLISTERS

Blisters are often a sign of ill-fitting shoes or the result of some unaccustomed activity. There is not much you can do about them.

Try not to pick at a blister. The outer layer of skin over the blister protects the sensitive inner layers beneath. If the bubble of fluid is large and taut, it can be lanced with a needle which you should first sterilise by heating in a flame.

A small crop of blisters may appear if you are allergic to something that you have come into contact with (see ALLERGY, p. 9). A mild, soothing cream (such as calamine lotion) is the best treatment. You should obviously try to avoid touching the substance which caused the trouble, otherwise the rash may well appear again.

There are a number of very rare diseases which cause the skin to blister easily. These usually need treatment from a doctor.

BLUSHING

Blushing is a sign of embarrassment or emotion. There is nothing you can do about it except try not to let it bother you. If you are self-conscious about blushing, you will blush even more.

Blushing is a nuisance because it lets other people

know more about your feelings than you might want them to know. Also, it might make people think you are guilty of something when you are not. It can make you an easy person to tease. But as you become more sure of yourself, you will blush less often.

BODY ODOUR

Everybody has a body odour of some sort. This is because at puberty special sweat glands under the armpits and around the groin begin to produce a substance which has a slight odour. Depending on whether you are a boy or girl, this odour will differ. In either case, it is not unpleasant.

What is unpleasant is when this odour becomes stale. Some people take a bit of time to realise that they have started producing this substance, and that they need to wash more often than before. Equally, they may not realise that it is necessary to change their clothes more often than they did as a child.

So body odour (or BO) is just stale sweat. The only cure is to wash more often. Deodorants help by decreasing the amount of sweat produced, and talcum powders help further by drying up the sweat. But neither prevents sweat going stale and causing BO. Ideally, you should wash all over every day and change your shirts and underclothes as often as necessary.

BOILS AND CARBUNCLES

A boil is a spot of infection on the skin where pus collects. Groups of boils are called carbuncles.

Small boils are particularly likely to occur if you have acne (see p. 61). In this case, the skin should be kept scrupulously clean and the boils should not be picked, as this may damage the skin and cause scars. Let a boil come to a head naturally, even though it may become quite painful, and it will then burst and begin to heal.

Large, deep or frequently occurring boils should be

seen by a doctor, as different treatment may be needed. This is particularly true of infections on the fingers, which can spread and damage the muscles.

CHILBLAINS

These are itchy or painful red blotches which appear on the feet and/or hands during cold weather. You can best prevent them by wearing thick woollen socks or tights and gloves. If the chilblains are very troublesome, your doctor will be able to help.

COLD SORES

Cold sores on the lips are mainly a problem in childhood. They are caused by a virus infection (see p. 41), and will get better of their own accord in a few days. A little mild antiseptic cream may prevent them becoming infected and thus more painful.

Before the cold sore actually appears, you may be aware of a tingling sensation in the skin. If this is so, it may help to hold an ice cube against the area. The cold sore will still develop, but may be smaller and less persistent.

CORNS

Skin gets thicker if it is constantly rubbed. If you wear shoes which are tight-fitting or which put pressure on one part of the foot, the skin will get thicker in that place. If this thick skin becomes inflamed and sore, the result is a corn.

If you are developing corns, it is almost certain that your shoes do not fit properly. In order to avoid a lot of pain in a few years' time, you should throw out the offending shoes now. Wear loose-fitting shoes, and if you are worried by the appearance of your feet, consult a doctor or nurse for advice.

DANDRUFF

Skin is flaking off your body all the time. This is because it is constantly being replaced from underneath. If you wash regularly, you may well not have noticed this slow, gradual process. But if your skin is very dry, the flakes may become obvious. And if your scalp is dry, the flakes become visible as dandruff.

Your hair should be washed as often as is necessary to keep it in good condition. But overstrong shampoos, which are often used for greasy hair, can dry your scalp and cause dandruff. Try different shampoos until you find one that suits you.

Seborrheic dermatitis is a condition which causes bad dandruff and flaking scaly skin, particularly behind the ears and over the neck. There is no obvious cause for it, but it does get better with time. Lotions and special shampoos from a doctor will help.

EAR PIERCING

If you want pierced ears, go to a reputable beauty shop. Do not try to do it yourself. You will probably end up with infected ear lobes.

After the ear has been pierced, a stud is put in the lobe to keep the hole open. This must remain in for at least three weeks while a tunnel of skin grows down the newly-pierced hole. This hole will close up quickly and easily if the stud is removed, but once the tunnel of skin has grown, the hole will close only slowly, over a period of weeks, unless earrings are worn.

Sometimes the earlobe is bruised when it is pierced, and will swell up painfully. You should check that the stud is loose, and that there is no danger of the end of the stud slipping into the earlobe through the newly-pierced hole. If this should happen, it can be difficult to remove.

If the earlobe becomes infected, the stud will have to be taken out immediately. Both problems are more likely to occur with inexpert piercing and poor quality studs.

ECZEMA

This is a troublesome rash which occurs particularly in children and those with dry skin. It is a type of skin allergy (see p. 9), but the rash often comes and goes for no apparent reason. The skin becomes very itchy and looks red and scaly. It is difficult to resist scratching, but this irritates the skin and makes the eczema worse.

The eczema itself almost always improves with time, but the dry skin that may come with it can continue to cause trouble, particularly in cold weather. Creams and lotions from a doctor will help both problems.

FRECKLES

These are harmless spots of pigmentation (see p. 73) on the face and arms which often fade with age. They are more obvious in the summer because the ultraviolet light in the sun's rays brings out the brown pigment.

HAIR

The texture of your hair cannot be changed. Some people have coarse hair, some fine. Whether it curls naturally or not depends on the shape of the hair's roots, and this is unalterable.

Caring for your hair

Hair is fragile. Vigorous brushing, or pulling on it too hard when it is being plaited, will weaken it. Strong shampoos and frequent, prolonged use of blow-dryers will destroy the natural oils which keep hair supple and healthy.

Your hair needs enough washing to keep it clean from general dirt, and from excess natural grease. But the shampoo you choose should be weak enough not to dry out the natural oils in the scalp since, if these are lost, dandruff may result (see p. 67).

Hair growth

Each hair grows for about three years and then falls out. You have about 100,000 hairs on your head, and lose between twenty and fifty hairs every day quite naturally. Your hair will not fall out after a shock.

Nor will your hair suddenly change colour. 'Going grey overnight' is not possible. But people do, of course, go grey gradually as they get older.

Alopecia areata is a rare condition in which the sufferer has small areas of baldness. It usually gets better of its own accord. A very few people lose all their body hair with this disease.

Facial hair

Boys need to shave with increasing regularity from about a year after puberty. Some, especially those of Asian origin, may need to shave very infrequently.

Girls also grow a very small amount of hair on their upper lip. Usually, it is almost invisible, but sometimes it may be more visible than the girl likes. This is more likely if she is olive-skinned. The hair is not abnormal, and certainly does not mean the girl is becoming masculine.

Hair-removing creams or lotions will not remove this hair totally. At best, they will help only a little. Surgical treatment is expensive, and unless done very expertly, does not give a good result.

Sexual hair

This is coarser than the hair on your head. It begins to grow at puberty in the groin, as pubic hair, and in the armpits. The amount of body hair you have bears no relation to your sexual maturity or prowess, and varies greatly from person to person.

ITCHING

A mild itch is nothing to worry about. You probably scratch yourself many times each day without even realising it.

But a severe or persistent itch is more likely to be due to some skin problem. The cause may be obvious, such as a rash or an insect bite. Then calamine lotion will help to soothe the skin. Occasionally it is not. Usually, when you visit a doctor with itchy skin, he will be able to suggest a simple remedy. In any event, frequent scratching will only irritate the skin.

LICE

Head lice are quite common in young children, but apart from the unpleasant sensation of discovering insects in your hair, they do not cause any real harm. The lice lay eggs which stick to the hairs — so just washing the hair does not get rid of them.

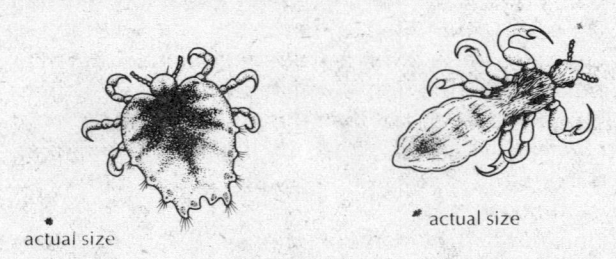

actual size   *actual size*

Different types of lice

Pubic lice, sometimes known as 'crabs', are another branch of the same family. You can catch them through sexual contact with an infected partner. Again, they are unpleasant without actually doing much harm.

There are special shampoos or lotions, available from chemists, which kill both types, but they must be used correctly if they are to work effectively. Do not be embarrassed to ask for a lotion if you cannot see it on the shelf.

MOLES

Moles are harmless spots of pigmented skin (see PIGMENTATION, p. 73) and most people have a few of them. If you have one which is prominent and catches on clothing, a doctor can easily remove it in a tiny operation using local anaesthetic. This leaves a small scar. Trying to remove it yourself will be painful and bloody and will not succeed.

If a mole suddenly becomes painful or starts to grow, you should see a doctor. He or she might feel it would be sensible to remove it.

NAILS

You should take good care of your nails. If treated badly, they look ugly and are liable to painful infections.

Brittle nails

Brittle fingernails can be a problem, especially if you have been slightly unwell for a month or so, or if you suffer from a skin complaint like psoriasis (see p. 73). Frequent varnishing of the nails will make the problem worse. The only answer is to cut them fairly short until they get stronger again.

Bruises under the nail

It is easy to bang your fingers or toes when doing heavy manual work. Sometimes a bruise or blood blister will form under the nail, and this is not only very painful, but may lead to the eventual loss of the nail. If the nail looks black and is still painful a few hours after you have hurt it, it will help to drain the blood from under the nail.

To do this, stick the head of a pin into a cork, and then heat the tip of the pin in a flame. Allow the red-hot tip to rest on the centre of the bruised nail, and, without pushing, let it burn through the nail. (You may need to

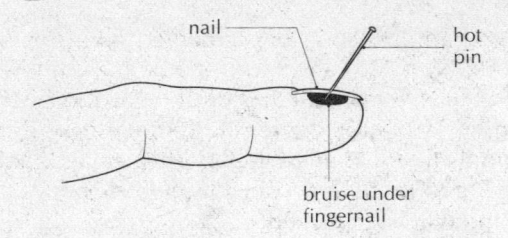

How to relieve the pain of a bruise under your fingernail

reheat it). When the pin gets through the nail, the blood will escape from the hole, cooling the hot needle. If the bruise was large, it will have separated the nail from its bed, and the nail will become loose and eventually drop off.

Ingrowing nails

An ingrowing toenail occurs when the edges of the nail cut into the side of the finger or toe and cause an infection. This happens when toenails are not cut across with straight scissors as they should be, or when the nail edges are bitten. If an ingrowing nail is very painful, it may need treatment from a doctor. If it occurs again and again, a small operation may be needed to stop it recurring.

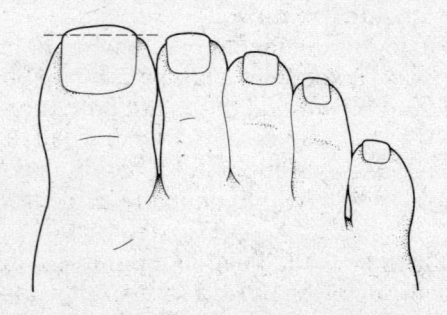

Cut your toenails straight across

Nail biting

Bitten nails do not look very elegant. Try to remember how revolting badly bitten nails look every time you are tempted to bite them and you may find it easier to break the habit. Alternatively, you can buy a special, colourless and foul-tasting liquid to paint on them. This is often highly effective. Nail biting can cause mild infections which may deform the nails.

PIGMENTATION

Almost everyone has melanin pigment in their skin. It is spread evenly through the skin surface and, in white people, becomes more obvious after sunbathing. Coloured people obviously have more of this pigment than white people. This is because they originally lived in hot countries and needed extra protection against the sun.

Freckles, moles and birthmarks all occur where this pigment is concentrated in small areas of skin.

Albinos

A very few people have no pigment at all in their skin. They are called albinos, and have to be careful going out in the sun, as they get sunburnt very easily.

Vitiligo

Some people have patches of skin with no pigmentation. This condition is called vitiligo. It is not caused by any disease or infection and there seems to be no obvious reason why it develops. There is no cure.

PSORIASIS

Psoriasis is a flaky, scaly rash which lasts for a few months at a time, but which may keep coming back. It is not infectious or dangerous, but it can be embarrassing because other people do not know what it is. The longer you have psoriasis, the less likely it is to get completely better.

The rash gets better and worse for no obvious reason, though any illness may bring it out. The most important thing is to try not to let it interfere with your social life. Do not let it get you down.

RASHES

Rashes have many different causes. Some of them have been given their own headings — acne, eczema, psoriasis and ringworm, for example.

Many other common diseases also have rashes. Chicken pox, measles and german measles are amongst the best known.

Dermatitis

Dermatitis is an itchy red rash which appears if you touch something which irritates your skin or which you are allergic to (see ALLERGY, p. 9). Some common culprits include the metal on bra straps, jewellery and watchstraps, and some of the chemicals in cosmetics and strong soaps. The only way to cure dermatitis is to avoid touching the substance which is causing it.

Nettlerash

Nettlerash is a blotchy white itchy rash, similar to the weals caused by the sting of nettles. It is caused by an allergic reaction to certain foods or drugs (see ALLERGY, p. 9). The skin may become puffy, especially round the eyes. If this is severe, you should see a doctor.

RINGWORM

Despite its name, ringworm is not a disease caused by a worm, but an infection caused by a fungus. The symptom is an unpleasant itchy rash which, though not dangerous, will usually need treatment from a doctor or chemist before it gets better.

SCABIES

Scabies is caused by tiny little insects, called mites, which live just under the skin. They are so small you cannot see them with the naked eye but you may just be able to see the tiny raised lines which mark where their burrows are. The main symptom is an intense itch.

Scabies is not actually dangerous, just unpleasant, and it can be fairly easily dealt with by bathing in a special lotion available from a doctor or chemist. It is not a sign of dirtiness or bad habits. Anybody can be unlucky enough to pick it up. The important thing is to get treatment to clear it up.

SCARS

Scars never completely disappear, but they do fade with time. A clean cut, such as an operation scar, may become almost invisible after a few years.

Big scars take six or nine months to settle. During this time, they are sometimes itchy and red. The more jagged or dirty the original cut, the more obvious the scar. After burns, the scarred skin improves for several years, though it will always be rather thin and pale.

Some scars, particularly burn scars, become more, rather than less visible. The scar slowly grows and becomes thick and lumpy. This is called a **keloid**. A keloid is difficult to get rid of, but it is not dangerous. It is not a cancer.

SUNBURN

Ultraviolet rays from the sun burn the skin. How easily you burn depends on how much brown pigment there is protecting your skin (see PIGMENTATION, p. 73) and how sensitive it is. So, if you are already suntanned, you will not burn easily. But if you sunbathe after the winter, without any protection, you will burn very easily.

Suntan oil absorbs the ultraviolet rays which would otherwise burn you. You can now buy these in varying strengths for different types of skin.

Sunburn is painful, and kills the surface layers of the skin, so that they peel several days later. Once you are burnt, there is no cure, although a soothing cream may ease the pain. Calamine lotion is a good one to use.

Sunstroke is caused by very bad sunburn – so never go to sleep under a really hot sun. In mild cases of sunstroke you feel sick and have a headache. The best thing to do then is to drink plenty of water and rest in a dark room. If you actually are sick, and feel very ill, call a doctor or go to a hospital casualty department.

TATTOOING

A tattoo is for ever. Although you may feel now that you will always love the person whose name you want to have tattooed on your arm, you may well feel differently in a few months' time. It could then be difficult to explain the tattoo to your new girl or boyfriend!

If you are determined to have a tattoo, go to a reputable shop. Unhygienic tattooists can spread very dangerous diseases, and are probably not the best artists.

Tattoos can be removed, usually by doing a skin graft operation under anaesthetic. It is difficult to arrange for this operation to be done under the national health service.

VERUCCAS AND WARTS

A verucca, or wart, is a little hard lump of skin which grows on the feet or hands. Both veruccas and warts are caused by the same troublesome virus. Warts (usually on the fingers) get better of their own accord within three months, although another wart may by then have started growing nearby.

Warts are funny things. They may be troublesome for

months, and then suddenly disappear for no obvious reason. A doctor can try to get rid of them by freezing them off, but they may not want to go. Your grandmother's cure using toads, or mushrooms at midnight, may work rather better!

Veruccas are more persistent than warts, because your weight treads them into the skin of the sole of the foot. They may become large and quite painful. It is only fair to get treatment from a doctor or chemist as soon as possible, since they are mildly infectious. Do not walk around barefoot while you have them, and keep your feet dry by using talcum powder.

Warts on the penis and vulva are spread during sex (see SEXUALLY TRANSMITTED DISEASES, p. 147). It is important to see a doctor about these before they grow too large. They are different from ordinary warts. There is no chance of a finger wart spreading to your genitals.

WHITLOWS

These are small infections, like bad acne spots (see p. 61), which occur in the flesh at the edge of the fingernails. They are painful, and if they do not settle quickly it is important to see a doctor or nurse since the infection can spread and damage the finger.

3
Diet, Food and Growth

ANOREXIA NERVOSA

This condition is much more common among girls than boys. It usually affects those who are very conscious about their weight, and who have put themselves on a very strict diet. Some even go to the extent of hiding food or making themselves sick. After a while, their health begins to break down. Unfortunately, most people with anorexia do not realise they are harming themselves. If a friend of yours is behaving strangely about food, do tell a teacher, your school nurse or a doctor.

Anorexia nervosa is fairly easily treated in the early stages. So get advice from a nurse or doctor if you find that you are worrying all the time about your weight.

If you have anorexia you must learn to accept and understand the condition. Most people who have it keep pretending that there is nothing wrong. Nobody will attempt to force-feed you. And it is important to get treated before the condition makes you really unwell.

CALORY

All food contains energy, and the amount of energy in food is measured in calories. Most adults use about 3,000 calories each day. Young people, unless very active, need rather less. You use more energy with exercise, and in cold weather. Also the heavier you are, the more energy you need to keep going.

If you eat more calories in your food than you need, the extra energy is stored as fat and you put on weight. If you eat less than you need, you lose weight.

If you know the calory content of your food, you can plan a diet which will give you more or less energy, according to whether you want to put on or take off weight. There are books you can buy which give the exact calory content of all foods and these may be useful.

CARBOHYDRATE

Carbohydrate is the scientific word which describes the sugary or starchy content of foods. Foods with lots of carbohydrate make up the bulk of your diet, and so cutting down on carbohydrate is one way of losing weight.

All sugars are carbohydrate, so cakes, sweets and chocolate are all fattening. Vegetable foods, such as potatoes, peas, and the flour in bread, also consist mainly of carbohydrate.

DIET BALANCE

You cannot be healthy without having a balanced diet. Carbohydrate, fats, fibre, protein and vitamins (see pp. 80, 82, 82, 89, 89) are all essential.

Carbohydrate provides the energy-rich bulk of food, which satisfies hunger. Fats also provide a good energy source. Fibre helps your digestion and keeps the bowels functioning properly. Protein is essential for growth and for keeping fit. Many different vitamins are needed, but only in very small amounts; they keep the body's nerves and muscles working smoothly. All of these are present in a normal healthy diet.

Fresh food is preferable to stored or pre-cooked food because the storage or cooking process can destroy

carbohydrate and fats

+

protein

+

essential vitamins and fibre

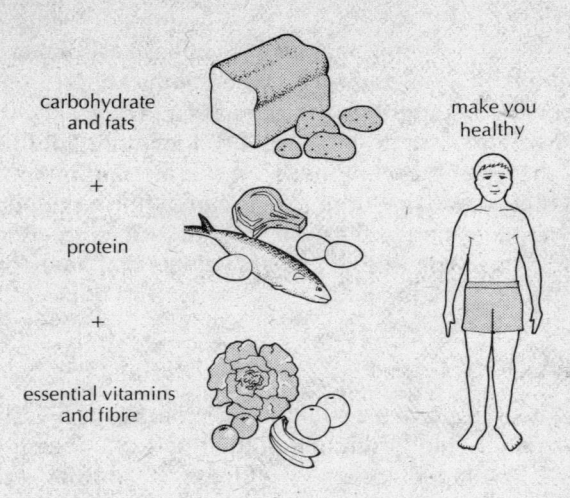

make you healthy

some of the food's goodness. This is especially true of vegetables, and the vitamins in them.

DIETING

Sensible people eat the amount of food they need to keep their weight steady. Ideally they are neither underweight, nor overweight.

Very few young people ever need to follow a really strict diet. Avoiding energy-rich foods like chips and sweets, and cutting out snacks is usually sufficient.

If you think your diet is fattening, and you want to change it to a healthier one with less energy calories in it, all you need to do is cut down on any foods which contains fats (see p. 82), such as greasy chips and fried food. To compensate, eat more foods which are bulky and high in fibre content, such as granary bread, bran cereals, green vegetables and fruits. If you can eat fewer foods with carbohydrate in them (see p. 80), such as bread and potatoes, you will be surprised to find how much easier it is to control your weight.

It is always easier not to put weight on, than to take it off. For this reason it is better to eat a large breakfast than a large supper. The energy you take in at breakfast is worked off through the day, whereas the energy from supper is stored through the night as fat.

If you are trying to lose weight, it is important that your diet is a balanced one. So if you are starting on a long diet, get advice from a dietician or nurse. You do not want to get an unpleasant vitamin deficiency. And anorexia nervosa (see p. 79) is an illness that anybody can get.

DWARVES

True dwarves have a condition called **achondroplasia** which is inherited from one of their parents. They are normal intelligent people, with the misfortune that their legs and arms are not in proportion with the rest of their body.

FATS

(If you are worried about being too fat, see OVER-WEIGHT, p. 86.)

Fats can make food taste nice. Unfortunately, fats also contain a lot of energy, or calories (see p. 79), and too many calories make you fat. If you need to lose weight, first cut down on fried foods, and on foods which are oily or which contain cream. Some of the most common are butter, fatty meats and chips. Vegetable oil margarines are probably healthier than butter, but are no less fattening.

FIBRE

Fibre, or roughage, is the fibrous part of your diet, which is neither digested nor absorbed. It passes straight through the body and makes up the bulk of your bowel motion each morning.

Fibre satisfies hunger without providing the calories

(see p. 79), which make you put on weight. Bran cereals, granary bread, green vegetables and fruit all contain fibre.

Modern convenience foods do not have much fibre in them. This is unhealthy because the digestion is prevented from working as well as it should. Also, there is less bulk to the morning's bowel motions. Indigestion (see p. 39) and constipation (see p. 22) are often the result.

It is likely that a diet which is high in fibre will protect you from some serious diseases and cancers in later life.

FOOD HYGIENE

This is essential. You will not be popular if you poison your family with food you have not prepared properly!

Food bacteria

To understand how food poisoning can occur, it is necessary to know something about the germs which cause it. These germs are called bacteria. Most types of bacteria are harmless, but some cause disease. The bacteria which cause food poisoning grow on food. Bacteria germs are very good at slipping into the kitchen: they blow in the wind; they stick to the feet of insects, which fly from dustbin to fruit bowl; they hide under fingernails and on bits of dirt. They grow best in warm, moist places, although they are killed by strong heat.

But if you take these simple precautions the germs will find it difficult to get at your food:

*1 Store all perishable foods in the fridge or larder
*2 Keep all food covered
*3 Keep all food dry
*4 Make sure that your hands, and any kitchen implements you are going to use, are clean before you touch any food

Contaminated foods

Despite these precautions, it is impossible to stop some foods from going stale. We all know what milk and bread look like when they have gone 'off'. They look like this because bacteria germs have grown in them, making them inedible.

Even if you cook food which has gone 'off', it is not safe to eat. This is because as bacteria grow, they produce a poison not unlike our urine. Humans become ill if they eat food contaminated by this poison.

So precautions are needed to stop us eating contaminated food:

*1 Do not keep perishable food for more than three days
*2 Store all food carefully
*3 Make sure all food is cooked thoroughly. Cooking kills germs before they have a chance to grow
*4 Once the food is cooked, do not keep it too long. After it has been reheated once, throw it away

This last point is important. Neither cooked food, nor shellfish look contaminated, even when they are quite poisonous. Cooked rice, which has been reheated, and slightly stale shellfish are the commonest causes of food poisoning.

FOOD STORAGE

Stored food nearly always goes 'off' because it has become contaminated. To prevent food going stale, it must either be completely protected from germs, or it must be kept in a form which discourages germs from growing.

Tinned and packaged foods are obviously completely protected from contamination.

Bacteria germs cannot grow without moisture. So flour, sugar, herbs, dried fruit (such as raisins) and everything else commonly kept in jars is safe. Deep frozen food is also dry, and will keep well unless defrosted.

Bacteria germs cannot grow happily if certain chemicals are in the food. Vinegar (pickled onions), salt (salt beef) and smoke (as in smoked salmon) all protect food for a time.

Bacteria germs do not like the cold. Most foods will last longer in a fridge.

But even if food is well protected from germs, it will eventually go stale. It is impossible to keep food for ever. Even tinned food lasts only a few years. Items like bread last only a few days.

HEIGHT

The average height for man and woman is different in every country. There is no ideal height and people vary considerably. For instance, most boys and girls on their thirteenth birthday are between 4' 6" (132 cms) and 5' 6" (168 cms). But one in twenty quite normal children are outside even this wide range.

It is extremely rare for someone to be very tall or very small for any other reason than that their parents are tall or small. A spurt of growth occurs at puberty, but as this may occur as early as ten or as late as seventeen, big differences in height during these years often become less obvious later on.

A very uncommon condition called **gigantism** is caused by a hormone upset during growth. This also causes other problems which your doctor will be able to advise you about if you are worried.

There is no doubt that tall people find it easier to get attention from other people. Whether they are worth listening to, is of course a completely different question! But it does seem likely that high heels will remain fashionable, and that policemen will wear helmets for some time to come.

MALNUTRITION

Malnutrition may be caused by eating too little of everything. Alternatively, it may be caused by missing out an essential part of a normal healthy diet (see DIET BALANCE, p. 80).

Food shortage
Malnutrition caused by a shortage of food occurs in many of the underdeveloped countries of the world. Apart from the terrible suffering it inflicts, malnutrition also prevents the bodies and minds of starving children from growing and developing as well as they should.

Yet there is sufficient food in the world for everyone. So-called developed nations eat far more than their fair share of the world's food. Underdeveloped countries are usually not rich enough to buy food from abroad. Even when they get it, they often have great problems with its storage and distribution. In the event of a disaster, such as war, crop failure or flood, thousands of people may starve before help arrives.

Diet deficiency
Malnutrition caused by the lack of an important part of a normal diet can occur even in developed countries. For example, pensioners who live on their own often eat almost nothing but fried foods and may develop vitamin deficiencies. This is because the process of frying destroys some vitamins (see p. 89).

Rickets and **scurvy** are examples of conditions caused by deficiencies of vitamin D and vitamin C respectively.

OVERWEIGHT

The painter Rubens painted most of his beautiful ladies with distinctly plump figures. And in parts of the Middle East, a man likes his wife to be fat because it implies that he can afford to feed her properly.

But, generally speaking, the fashionable and health-conscious modern girl (and boy) is expected to be slim.

Putting on weight
Girls often put on weight (so-called puppy fat) during their teenage years. Girls who are taking the contraceptive pill may also find that their weight increases. Both boys and girls often put on weight if they start working in an office, where they spend most of the time sitting down, or if they suddenly stop playing sport.

Why do you put on weight?
Food is eaten. It contains energy. Energy is used as fuel for exercise and to keep you warm. Any unused energy is stored as fat. In other words, you put on weight. Regular exercise will use up energy and help keep your weight down.

Fat people have efficient bodies, which use energy sparingly; thin people burn off surplus energy and do not get fat. It is all rather unfair! Losing weight is difficult for a naturally fat person, so it is better not to put on weight in the first place. This means being weight-conscious. Everything you eat has energy in it. Be aware of what you eat and how fattening it is (see CALORY, p. 79).

Losing weight
Being very fat is not pleasant. Sore areas develop easily between skin folds of fat, and the extra weight causes back strain. You are also slightly more likely to develop artery disease in later life (see p. 154). Exercise does not appeal because it is not much fun exposing yourself to ridicule.

There is no easy magic cure for being fat. Eating less is the only sure way to lose weight. If you want a specific diet to follow there are many good ones to be found in magazines and books. But remember that it is far better to go on a long-term diet, cutting your food intake gradually, than to crash diet for two weeks, then eat just as much as before. Regular exercise helps. Walk or cycle to school or to work, instead of catching a bus; when indoors, try to stay active instead of slumping in a chair.

Treatment with tablets or operations is not usually the answer. Being overweight is not a disease, and doctors cannot 'cure' it. The person concerned simply has to learn to eat less and do more. In the long run, this is the only answer.

Overweight children often become overweight grown-ups. A sympathetically organised diet started in early life may save much misery later on. But if someone you know is plump do not tease them about their size. Teasing will only make them unhappy and tempt them to take comfort from eating something fattening.

POSTURE

It is very easy to give good advice about posture, but very few people actually take any notice.

Any position which puts a persistent strain on the back is liable to cause backache. Once you have backache, the damage caused by poor posture has already begun.

When sitting, the backbone should be straight, not bent into the comfortable slouching curve your back is probably in at the moment! Your bottom should be close to the back of the chair.

When standing, the head should be erect on the shoulders, not dropping forwards like a wilting daffodil. Girls whose breasts are developing, or who are tall, may slouch because they are embarrassed about their appearance. But girls, and boys, look more attractive if they stand up straight.

When working for a long period, either sitting or standing, make sure that you are not uncomfortable and that your work-surface is above hip level.

PROTEIN

Protein is part of a healthy diet and is essential for growth. A balanced diet must contain a certain amount of protein. Most animal and dairy products are rich in protein.

Extra protein has neither aphrodisiac nor brain-expanding powers.

ROUGHAGE (see FIBRE, p. 82)

VITAMINS

Vitamins are complicated chemicals, which your body needs, but is unable to make for itself. They are an essential part of a healthy diet. Most vitamins are needed in only very small amounts, but they are essential if different parts of the body are to work properly.

For example, vitamin A is needed by the eye. Without it, you would not be able to see. A shortage of this vitamin is a frequent reason for blindness in some countries.

Vitamin C is sometimes recommended to stave off colds. It does no harm, but probably does little good either.

Some vitamins are actually poisonous in large quantities. It is unwise to take lots of vitamin pills, unless advised to do so by a doctor.

WEIGHT

It is impossible to say exactly how much you should weigh. The thickness of your bones, the size of your head, the shape of your body, and your height all help to determine your weight. A chart can only give a very average weight for your height.

Most people can tell if they are overweight fairly easily. Strip off, and stand in front of a mirror. Look at yourself critically. Pinch a thickness of skin and surface fat on your tummy, or bottom, between your finger and thumb.

If you can easily pinch out a thickness of skin and fat which is several centimetres thick, you probably need to lose a bit of weight. You will also probably look rather plump in the mirror.

If you have to stretch your skin to get a pinch between finger and thumb, or if you can only pinch out a double thickness of skin, you are clearly not overweight. You certainly should not be dieting (see also OVERWEIGHT, p. 86).

4
Drugs and Medicines

Drugs and medicines, if used sensibly, can give great benefit. But all medicines should be used only when necessary. There are no medicines which are useful which do not occasionally have troublesome side-effects (see p. 101). If you are starting on a new drug, ask your doctor if there are any side-effects you should look out for.

Some people obtain drugs and take them purely for their own enjoyment. This is not only against the law, but also highly dangerous.

How to get drugs and medicines

Certain tablets and medicines can be bought from a chemist as and when you need them. But the majority must be obtained through prescription. This means getting a signed prescription from a doctor to take to a chemist.

When collecting medication from a chemist, make sure you know when to take it. For instance, the contraceptive pill should be taken daily; antibiotics should be taken every day for as long as is directed; other treatments may only need to be taken when you feel you need them.

ADDICTION

An addict is someone who is unable to get through the day without taking the drug to which they are addicted.

Many adults take sleeping tablets every night. Perhaps your mother or father does. If they run out of tablets they may hardly notice. However, if they become jittery and unable to sleep, they are probably addicted – although they would probably strongly deny it.

This type of addiction is very common. And people can also become addicted to tea, coffee, nerve tablets, cigarettes and alcohol.

Some more serious types of addiction change the way the brain and other organs work. For instance, if you drink several alcoholic drinks in quick succession, you will become sleepy-drunk. This effect wears off after a few hours, and leaves no lasting damage. But an alcoholic drinks heavily every day. Their body gets used to the alcohol. If they stop drinking, their brain keeps on sending 'stay awake' messages which counteract the sleepy-making alcohol. Without alcohol they become jittery and shaky.

They may become so nervous and fidgety that they start seeing things and behaving very strangely. This reaction is known as the DTs (delirium tremens). They have to have another drink. They are an alcohol addict (see ALCOHOLISM, p. 94).

Smoking

The nicotine in cigarettes also has a calming effect. A heavy smoker 'needs' a cigarette after a night's sleep without cigarettes. The first cigarette of the day soothes the jittery feeling a cigarette addict experiences.

Hard drugs

The so-called hard drugs, heroin and morphine, are also addictive. But they are much more dangerous than alcohol or cigarettes because they stop you thinking about anything except the drug and its effects. So if the drug is being used every day, the addict does not eat or take care of himself. Heroin addicts often die of self-neglect.

ALCOHOL

Although many people find one or two drinks enjoyable and relaxing, alcohol is a drug and should be treated with respect.

The amount of alcohol you can drink without becoming drunk depends upon your size and how often you have had alcohol before. Normally, the younger you are, the less you are able to drink. A glass of milk, or a meal, before drinking reduces the effect of the alcohol by delaying its absorption into the body.

The first effect of alcohol is to remove inhibitions. It makes you less shy and more outgoing. It makes you feel more confident. At the same time, it gradually makes you sleepier. Because of the first effect, the second may go unnoticed. This is why driving after even one drink is dangerous. Sleepiness and over-confidence are a lethal combination.

Drunkenness is not only dangerous when driving. Every year, people kill themselves by drinking too much too quickly. They go to sleep, are then sick, and drown in their own vomit.

If you are with someone who has fallen asleep while drunk, make sure that they are lying on their side — *not* flat on their back. If you cannot rouse them at all, call a doctor and stay with them until he or she arrives.

Some people do not go to sleep when they are drunk. They become very uninhibited or violent. In this state it is easy to do something stupid you might be sorry for later on. But it is too late for apologies or remorse if you are in prison, or waiting for your child to be born.

Alcohol is a taste you either like or dislike, like any other. If you do not like it there is nothing to be ashamed of. Do not drink just because your friends do.

ALCOHOLISM

Heavy drinking over a long time not only stops you working properly and breaks up your friendships, it also damages your health. Liver problems (cirrhosis) often occurs in alcoholics. This makes them feel very ill and they may become jaundiced (see p. 42). Alcohol, together with vitamin deficiencies, will damage the brain (see MALNUTRITION, p. 86), and this is why some alcoholic down-and-outs behave so strangely even when not drunk.

Nobody thinks they are an alcoholic! And it is very difficult to say when social drinking becomes alcoholism. But anybody who drinks secretively, who 'needs' a drink, or whose drinking disrupts their life (because of hangovers or drunkenness), is certainly an alcoholic (see ADDICTION, p. 91).

How to cope with an alcoholic parent

Many children who have an alcoholic father or mother feel very helpless. It is difficult to know how to help the alcoholic, especially if he or she does not want help.

Often it may seem easiest simply to accept the heavy drinking and to try and control the embarrassing behaviour. But the alcoholic will almost certainly get worse in time and may become very ill. If young children are involved, or if the family is suffering because of violence or lack of money, you should seek help. Do not suffer in silence.

Talk about the problem with a relative or teacher that you trust. Your doctor will also be quite happy to talk confidentially about family problems, and may be able to suggest an organisation which can help you.

Alcoholics who want to control their drinking can get a lot of help from an organisation called Alcoholics Anonymous. Their telephone number is in the telephone directory.

ANTIBIOTICS

Antibiotics can be taken in the form of tablets, medicines or injections. There are many different kinds, including penicillin, ampicillin, erythromycin, septrin and tetracyclines. These are all life-saving drugs used to combat serious diseases such as pneumonia and meningitis (see pp. 44 and 45).

Antibiotics work by killing the bacteria germs which cause infection. They do not kill virus germs. Antibiotics clear up chest infections, urinary infections, and some throat infections. These infections are caused by bacteria germs. Colds, flu and diarrhoea are all caused by virus germs. They cannot be cured by antibiotics.

It takes time to kill all the germs. So you should take the antibiotics for as long as your doctor tells you. A course of antibiotics *must* be completed. Otherwise the infection may only half clear up, and cause worse trouble later.

Antibiotics are very safe. But girls on the contraceptive pill risk becoming pregnant if they take antibiotics as well. This is because the pill may not work properly. You should take extra precautions if you have intercourse when taking antibiotics and the pill.

ANTI-DEPRESSANTS

Feeling depressed is something we all experience from time to time. If you have failed in some way or if a friendship has broken up, it is natural to be miserable. But this depression will almost certainly pass reasonably quickly. But if someone becomes depressed about being depressed, a vicious circle quickly develops which will not allow them to shake off the feeling. When this happens, they are suffering from the illness called depression.

A doctor may then feel that anti-depressant tablets will help. They need to be taken for at least a month. Although they may not solve the problem causing the depression, they usually allow the patient to see things in a more cheerful and positive light. The patient may then be able to work out the problem for themselves.

ANTIHISTAMINES

These are commonly used tablets which help to relieve most types of allergic reaction (see ALLERGY, p. 9). They are particularly useful to hay fever sufferers. But antihistamines do have the disadvantage of making you feel sleepy. This can often make the treatment more trouble than it is worth.

DRUG ABUSE (see also ADDICTION, p. 91)

It is very easy to start experimenting with drugs, especially if your friends are using them. It is much less easy to stop. Drugs can quickly become a way of life.

Drugs become a habit which destroys your family ties and ruins your prospect for a happy life. They make you feel helpless and unhappy until you take the next dose. They are also very expensive.

Those who experiment with drugs think that they will not get caught by the police, that the drugs will not make them ill, and that they will never become 'hooked'. Unfortunately, police stations and hospitals are crowded with people who have discovered that this is not true.

Amphetamines

Amphetamines keep you awake and make you feel overexcited and excessively lively.

Amphetamines are addictive because this more lively personality is difficult to give up. Yet although they make you feel good, they upset your concentration and make logical thought difficult. This is why amphetamines are not helpful when studying for exams or working late into the night.

Home-made amphetamines are often contaminated, and can be very dangerous indeed.

Barbiturates
Barbiturates are sedatives (this means that they have a calming effect). They are sometimes prescribed as sleeping tablets. A barbiturate addict has a sleepy, rather pointless existence. It is easy to start on barbiturates, but it is much more difficult to stop because they are very addictive.

Cannabis
Cannabis has many names which change with local custom and with the appearance of the cannabis leaf preparation. It may be called hash, marihuana, weed, leaf or many other names.

Cannabis is made from the leaves of the cannabis plant, and it is usually mixed with tobacco and smoked. It makes you feel rather dizzy, but also contented and relaxed.

Excessive smoking of cannabis is harmful, but medically speaking its occasional use is probably no more dangerous than other more socially acceptable drugs, such as alcohol or nicotine. Cannabis is illegal, and has no useful medical use.

Cocaine
Cocaine is a white powder which is usually sniffed. It keeps you awake and makes you feel excited. It often makes your nose feel extremely itchy. Occasionally it can cause a quite severe, but shortlasting mental breakdown.

Heroin
Heroin is a very powerful drug made from poppy seeds. In hospitals it is injected to soothe the severe pains of heart attacks and cancers. If used without medical supervision, it is a very dangerous drug indeed.

Heroin produces a euphoria so heady that ordinary

life quickly seems flat and uninteresting in comparison. The drug is highly addictive so that the user soon loses interest in everything else (see ADDICTION, p. 91).

As time goes by, addicts need more and more heroin to get the same effect. If they do not get the drug, they suffer extremely unpleasant withdrawal symptoms.

Heroin addicts can be cured, but quite a large number die. The temptation to start back on the drug never goes.

LSD

This powerful, and very dangerous, drug is almost always illegally manufactured. Many LSD tablets are contaminated as a result. Even in its pure form, it is a very dangerous drug to experiment with. An LSD 'trip' may be either a pleasant, or a horrifying experience, since the drug takes control of your mind, removing all sense of time and space.

LSD can bring on a severe mental breakdown (see p. 111). Never give it to anyone without their knowledge.

Sniffing

Sniffing glue or household liquid detergents is a highly dangerous and anti-social habit. The sensations it can produce are those of sleepiness, dizziness or confusion, depending on the substance. The effects are certainly not worth the risk.

Regular sniffing can cause severe brain damage. It can also harm the liver and lungs. Strong acids or bleaches will burn the skin. Sniffing in a confined space can make you suffocate.

If you want to stop sniffing but do not have a relative or teacher that you can trust for advice, go and see your doctor.

Tranquillisers

As you might guess, tranquillisers make you tranquil and sleepy. They are mildly addictive and, if taken frequently, can make you feel very depressed.

The drug habit

If you are taking drugs for kicks, have you ever stopped to wonder why you are taking them? Is it because your friends are doing it? Or is it because it seems exciting to break the law? Whatever the reason, you are putting your health and your future at risk. Make the decision to stop *now*. If you think you have not got the strength to stop by yourself, get help from a parent, teacher or doctor.

If a friend of yours is experimenting with drugs it is your responsibility to try and get them to stop. Is it because they want to impress other people or are they just bored? Try to understand why they are doing it. Make an effort to interest them in things which are not related to their drug habit. Persuade them to avoid the more dangerous experiments.

Most importantly, do not lose touch. Even if you are beginning to feel helpless and rejected, keep giving them a contact with their old way of life, away from coffee bars or pubs and their new circle of friends. Most people realise the futility of escape through drugs after a time.

OVERDOSE

One of the most popular ways of trying to commit suicide is to take an overdose of drugs. This can happen to even the most sensible person. So if anyone threatens suicide take it seriously. You should destroy or hide any tablets in the house, and try to talk through the problems causing the trouble.

Most people who take overdoses do not really intend to end their lives, although they may think so at the time. They are usually too upset to know how to get help from their family or friends.

The commonest drugs taken in overdose are painkillers and sleeping tablets. Painkillers usually contain paracetamol and this is not a drug which kills quickly or painlessly. It can cause liver damage and a lingering yellow jaundice (see p. 42).

If you discover somebody who has just taken an overdose, you should get them quickly to hospital. Make sure that the tablet wrappers and bottles go with the patient to hospital. In hospital, the patient will probably have a stomach washout. This means that a tube is passed down into the throat, and the inside of the stomach is washed out with jugs of water. This is not a pleasant procedure.

If the patient refuses to go to hospital, or there is likely to be a delay of three hours or more, it may help to make the patient sick. This should not be done if they are very drowsy or unconscious. Do not give them salty water to drink, as this can be very dangerous. A tablespoon of soapy washing-up liquid in a glass of water will usually do the trick.

PAINKILLERS

Aspirin and paracetamol are good painkillers. They soothe most headaches, joint pains and muscle sprains. Almost all brands of shop-bought painkillers are based on one of these two drugs. Both are very safe unless taken more often than directed on the packet.

Stronger painkilling tablets or even injections can be prescribed by a doctor. Unfortunately, the strongest painkillers, such as morphine, are very addictive (see p. 91). They are reserved for patients with heart trouble or cancers.

SEDATIVES

Valium and librium are two of the most commonly used sedatives. They are usually given to people who are worried or anxious about something and who need calming down. Usually they only need to be taken for a few days.

SIDE-EFFECT

A side-effect is an unwanted symptom or problem caused by a medicine. All medicines can have troublesome side-effects.

Some side-effects are quite dangerous. Most are merely inconvenient. Antihistamines, for example, which are used against hay fever, often cause sleepiness; antibiotics and iron tablets may lead to stomach upsets. It is a doctor's job to decide if taking a drug will do more harm than good. Generally speaking, the stronger and more effective the tablet, the more likely it is that a doctor will have to keep checking for side-effects.

People on the contraceptive pill, on hormone tablets, or on anti-cancer drugs, or those having treatment for blood pressure or arthritis need regular check-ups.

SLEEPING PILLS

Sleeping pills are overused. Nobody should expect a perfect night's sleep every night, and it is pointless to worry about the occasional difficulty in getting to sleep. It only makes things worse!

If you are regularly finding it difficult to get to sleep, try having a hot bath and a warm drink before going to bed. Sleeping pills should only be taken as a last resort since they are slightly addictive.

STEROIDS

Steroids are powerful drugs which take away the effects of inflammation. They can be taken as a tablet, a cream, or in an inhaler. They are very useful if the inflammation is causing the problem, as in asthma, eczema or arthritis.

But inflammation is the body's defence against infection. For this reason, steroids should never be used against an infection. The infection will get worse. In particular, steroid creams should never be applied to skin infections.

Like many other strong drugs, steroids have dangerous side-effects, especially if they are used wrongly. If taken in large amounts, the face may become round and plump. This swelling goes down when the tablets are reduced.

The discovery of steroids as a means of fighting serious disease is one of the greatest medical triumphs of the twentieth century. They are literally life-saving drugs.

TOBACCO

Tobacco is one of the most harmful of the addictive drugs. Research has proved that smoking causes the death of most heavy smokers.

When you are young it is difficult to worry about diseases that might occur in later life, but every cigarette does cause damage, and all smokers should know the facts.

Smoking destroys the lungs. Even children who smoke will notice that they cough up more phlegm than non-smokers if they get a cold. Smokers cough more, and get short of breath more easily. Lung damage often leads to bronchitis (see p. 17).

Smoking causes lung cancer. A person who smokes twenty cigarettes a day is twenty times more likely to die of lung cancer than a non-smoker.

Smokers get some other cancers at an earlier age than non-smokers

Smoking is harmful during pregnancy. If a pregnant woman smokes, her baby will be smaller than it should be. Small babies are more likely to catch serious infections and are more easily damaged by a difficult birth.

Smoking harms the arteries in the body. Smokers are more likely to have heart attacks and to get artery disease (see pp. 163, 154).

Smokers who have diabetes (see p. 26) or a bad chest, will probably kill themselves by smoking. If a close relative has chest or heart trouble, a smoker is quite likely to develop the same trouble.

Tobacco causes damage to the body when it is inhaled. None of us can avoid inhaling some tobacco smoke, and smoke in the air particularly affects babies and young children. Anybody who smokes should think of other people, and only smoke when it will not annoy those around them.

Pipe and cigar smokers cannot avoid breathing smoke in, even if they do not inhale it. The more smoke inhaled from cigarettes, cigar or pipes, the greater the risk to your health.

There are other, more obvious reasons why smoking is not sensible. It is very expensive, it spoils your sense of taste, causes bad breath and stains your hands and fingers.

Do not be tempted into starting to smoke by your friends or by advertisements. If you are already smoking, think of what it is costing you (in every sense) and give up now.

5
Personality, Relationships and Mental Health

ADOLESCENCE
An adolescent is in the process of changing from being a child to being an adult. This maturing process affects all aspects of your life. In particular, it affects your sexuality, your perception of the world and your moral attitudes.

Sexuality
A child is sexually immature and has only a hazy idea of what sex is about. An adult is mature and more at ease with sex. An adolescent is learning about the pleasures, and the responsibilities, of sexual activity.

Becoming aware of your body and finding out about sex can be fun. But people do vary in their reactions to this process of discovery. Some find that these new, and often intensely pleasurable sensations occupy all their thoughts and energy for a time. Others find they are scarcely affected by them. Certainly, parents and teachers are likely to think that success in exams or in sport is more important than any new sexual interests.

Sexual maturity brings an intense awareness of your own personal feelings. It also makes you more sensitive to the appearance and character of others of your own age. You will find that certain things matter enormously, and you may need a lot of time alone to come to terms with your new understanding of life.

Your perception of the world

A child lives in the present. He or she does not make plans for the future, but relies heavily on his or her parents for guidance. An adult is independent, and usually has clear plans and ambitions for the future.

Throughout your adolescence you will find that you slowly become less dependent on the support and guidance of your parents. Some people find this an easy process, with parent and offspring almost always agreeing. Others find that upsetting arguments are common and that it becomes difficult to talk to their parents. However, even the worst problems have a way of sorting themselves out. Although the future will sometimes look black and gloomy, at other times it will appear rosy and exciting. This can be disconcerting to those who can only see an unromantic dirty pink!

Moral attitudes

Adolescence is a time when your attitudes to politics, religion and the law may become important to you. You may find that you have strong feelings about important issues like abortion and nuclear disarmament. You will certainly learn that there are no easy clear-cut answers.

Childhood friendships are strong, but the friendships of adolescence are often deeper and founded on great loyalty. They will often last for many years. But if your friends start to do things which you feel are wrong, do not let your love and loyalty towards them lead you into following their example.

FAMILY RELATIONSHIPS

Parents

However much you love your parents, there are times when they seem to be out of touch and to hold old-fashioned and unreasonable views — particularly where you are concerned! But remember that your parents were young once and felt just the same as you, whatever they say now. If they seem disapproving, they are probably just anxious about you and want to prevent you from making the same mistakes that they made.

But because so many things have changed — school, job prospects and general attitudes — the problems your parents faced are not the same as those you face. As a result, your parents may find it difficult to understand your point of view. This is the so-called generation gap. It is not caused by any shortage of love or affection, but will be made worse if parents or offspring refuse to compromise on what are usually unimportant issues. Remember that it is confusing for your parents to see you squabbling like a child one minute, and asking to be treated like an adult the next! Try to understand your parents' point of view and you will find it much easier to get on with them.

Brothers and sisters

A brother or sister can be a marvellous friend — or the most annoying person in the world. If you have younger brothers and sisters, you may well find that they become increasingly irritating as you get older and you lose interest in playing their games. An older brother or sister may be just as annoying because they persist in treating you like a child and exclude you from their circle of friends.

Unfortunately, there is little you can do to change either of these situations, apart from trying to be patient. Remember that your younger brother or sister may be feeling left out and rejected. Your older brother or sister may become more understanding if you explain your point of view.

Extended family

You may be one of those lucky people with an extended family consisting of grandparents, aunts, uncles and cousins. If you are, you will know that a large family can give tremendous comfort and support, and your relationship with a cousin or grandparent may well be one of the best things in your life.

However, a large family can also seem overbearing at times, and your relatives' interest in you and what you are doing may seem like interference. But try to remember that this interest is prompted by love and concern for your well-being. In any event, it is seldom wise to cut yourself off from your family.

Parental arguments and separation

Like everyone else, your parents will sometimes have arguments. Depending on their personalities, these will either develop into full-scale rows or be quickly smoothed over. If these disagreements have seemed more frequent recently, this is probably because you have become more perceptive. Maybe your parents feel that you are mature enough to understand the arguments and so do not need to hide them from you. This can be an uncomfortable compliment.

Remember that there are two sides to every argument. Nobody is ever completely right or completely wrong. Most arguments are based on previous disagreements, which you may not be fully aware of.

If your parents separate, it is natural for you to feel angry and upset. But unless you know of very good reasons why you should not see one of your parents, you should try to keep in touch with both. You have much to gain from both your mother and your father.

If your parents have separated, you may find that you inherit responsibilities which are hard to bear. Your younger brothers or sisters may need extra help and time, both with school work and just talking. The parent at home will feel unhappy and will probably be short of money for a time. It may take months for life to settle down again. Try not to get too angry. Keep in touch with other members of your family and with your friends. They will be a great support.

MENTAL HANDICAP

A mentally handicapped person often has a normal healthy body, but the development of their brain has been slowed for ever. They can never be fully intelligent adults. Despite this, many of them are charming, lovable people that can teach us a great deal.

The amount of damage to the developing brain varies. Some unfortunate children are very severely handicapped, being unable to talk or think for themselves at all. In others, the damage is only slight, although they will usually need help with their schooling.

Some people are mentally handicapped from birth. This may be due to an unavoidable fault in their early development. For instance, all children with Down's syndrome (see p. 28) are to some extent mentally handicapped.

Other people are mentally handicapped as a result of an accident or disease which affected them at birth or early on in their life.

Looking after the mentally handicapped

Looking after mentally handicapped people is an enormous task for parents. A caring society must give them all the help and support it can. Some parents are unable to cope with a severely handicapped child, either because they are simply not strong enough to lift or control their growing child, or because the strain of coping with them is destroying their own lives. In these cases a hospital or institution is necessary to provide the best possible care.

MENTAL ILLNESS

It is often very difficult to decide when someone is mentally ill. The borderline between oddness and madness is blurred. Why does one person have a nervous breakdown after a bad shock, while another carries on as if nothing has happened?

Mental illness can be divided into three categories. Minor upsets and breakdowns are very common (see below) and many of us will experience one at some stage in our lives. They are the so-called neurotic illnesses.

The second category is major breakdowns and madness, which consist of the psychotic illnesses (see next page). Fortunately, this type of illness is rare. During these illnesses, the sufferer loses touch with reality and usually needs help from a psychiatrist.

The third category is the mental failing which may occur in old age. However, like everybody else, old people can of course suffer from the illnesses in the first two categories.

Minor upsets and breakdowns (neurotic illnesses)

Living is hard work and everybody needs a bit of help now and then. Your uncle gives you some cash and you feel better. You give your mum an unexpected kiss and she feels happier, and so on.

But sometimes everything becomes too much to bear. The brain says, 'Stop, I want a rest.' What happens then depends entirely on your personality and your situation. Men can usually find an excuse for a few days off work. Their wife looks after them and they soon feel better. Women are more likely to go to a doctor for some tablets, or to talk the problem over with their mother and try to carry on.

Usually, both get better. But sometimes, the brain says, 'Stop, I am going to have a rest.' And whether you want to or not, you find yourself unable to carry on normally. This is very depressing and you may become tearful and nervous. You may also become oversensitive to the slightest criticism, real or imagined.

It is usually fairly easy to see why the trouble has

occurred. Overwork or family worries are often to blame. The treatment will depend on the severity of the nervous breakdown. Usually a good rest and possibly help from a doctor or psychologist will quickly sort out the problem. But should the sufferer become depressed about being depressed, or anxious about being anxious, they may get ill enough to need hospital treatment.

If somebody has an anxiety neurosis, it means that they are more anxious than they should be, given the situation. If they have a' phobia, they are more afraid than they should be, given the situation. If they have a depressive illness, they are more depressed than they should be, given the situation. You can see now it is difficult to say when somebody is mentally ill. It is normal to be anxious about exams, it is normal to be scared of spiders or snakes, and it is natural to be miserable when a close friend or relative dies.

Any of us could have an illness or an upset such as those described above. It is very important that if it happens to a friend of yours, you should help them over the trouble by keeping in touch with them and encouraging them to lead a normal life.

Major breakdowns and madness (psychotic illnesses)

People who are psychiatrically mad cannot think logically. For this reason they are unable to behave normally. But, having said this, it can still be difficult to decide if a person is psychotic. You are certainly not mad if you think that the world is flat, and you are not necessarily mad if you are convinced that little green martians are after you with laser guns. It could possibly be true! Madness is like living in a very disjointed dream, or in the delirium of a fever.

If you meet someone who is mentally disturbed, never tease or frighten them. This sort of behaviour makes it even more difficult for them to think logically. Talk to them calmly about subjects that are very familiar. Keep them and yourself occupied by doing something routine like making a cup of tea. Remember what it is like for you when you have a nightmare. Then, as they gradually calm down (and this may take some time), they will find it easier to understand what is happening around them.

Mania
One form of madness is called mania. The sufferer is abnormally cheerful, thinks too fast and tries to do too much. Because they are thinking so fast, they cannot think logically. If they also have periods of being very miserable, they have a manic-depressive syndrome. Mania and related illnesses are treated very successfully with special drugs.

Schizophrenia
The other main form of madness is schizophrenia. A schizophrenic is not a double (or split) personality, as is popularly thought. An untreated schizophrenic cannot think logically because their thoughts are split from their personality and then jumbled up. This sounds complicated, and it is! The schizophrenic may hear voices and talk to people who do not exist.

The disease is treatable. Certain drugs help to re-arrange their thoughts and they start thinking logically again. The treatment may need to be continued for some months, or even years.

Schizophrenics are usually fairly solitary people who get confused and upset by too much talk. They often live on their own or with parents. They are not in any way dangerous or violent.

Mental health in old age
The elderly can have breakdowns, just like anybody else. Phsyical illness may also cause an old person to become confused or depressed. So if an old person becomes abnormally sleepy or forgetful, a doctor should be called to see them. Do not just put the

trouble down to old age.

Senility A more distressing and untreatable form of mental illness in old people is senility. This is a slow deterioration in their memory. Their ability to cope in situations needing thought (such as cooking and shopping) also gets worse.

Most children have good memories and are quick to learn. Adults find it harder to learn, but have a lot of experience to help them manage their daily lives. Old people find it harder still to learn, and also have difficulty in remembering things and in using the experience of their younger days.

The age at which old people's brains begin to slow up varies considerably. There are people over 100 years old who are bright and chirpy, and completely clear-headed. On the other hand, there are 65-year-olds who are incapable of living alone because they are so confused and vague.

The elderly become set in their ways. They dislike sudden changes in their life. If they have to move house or go on holiday, they are likely to need much longer than a younger person to plan the event, and to get used to the change. They may even find family visits rather taxing, however much they love their relatives.

If an old person has a tendency to become confused, this tendency becomes more noticeable if they are with strangers or in unfamiliar places.

Of course most old people can cope perfectly well alone. But by the age of eighty or so many of them need help at home. Cooking, cleaning and shopping become difficult. There may be dangers with cookers, fires and cigarettes.

In the later stages of the illness, their behaviour may become very distressing. They may behave unpredictably, going for walks or removing clothing at odd times. This often means that unless the person concerned has a close relative who is prepared to spend most of their life looking after them, they will need to be looked after in a home.

OLD PEOPLE

Nobody likes to think of themselves as old. But all of us get old eventually. Despite their extra years, old people have the same feelings and emotions as younger people.

One of the problems about getting old is the feeling of uselessness many people have. When they retire (men at sixty-five, women at sixty), they may feel that they have lost status and, in their eyes, their usefulness to society. Most people develop hobbies or interests, living with zest, but others need encouragement if they are not to sit down and die.

Grandparents tend to think of their grandchildren as their hope for the future. They want to be friends with them, but at the same time, they are not always prepared for the demands of a friendship with a young person. It is easy for older adults to look on young children as just part of their parents; it is not so easy when those children have opinions of their own!

Old people do become set in their ways, and they like to do things for themselves. Their pride may prevent them from showing the love for you that they really feel. You will probably find that in your relationships with older people, it is you who has to respect their wishes. This is how it should be. You have your strength and independence. They have their pride and experience.

PERSONALITY

Your personality is partly inborn, and partly shaped by your experiences. Here are a few of the traits which go up to make the essential 'you'.

Appearance
As soon as you meet someone, you start getting clues about what that person is like. Their hairstyle, clothes, expression and manner all tell you something.

It is particularly important to give a good impression at a job interview or at a party. Anybody who is attractive and stylishly dressed will have the edge over their competitors.

Job applications If an employer is looking for, say, a shop assistant, they will want someone who looks smart and shows interest in selling things. They will not take on someone who looks bored and is untidily dressed. Since it may be difficult to be genuinely enthusiastic about the article you might be selling, you have to pretend you are.

Try to forget any previous rejections, and throw off any slight depression you might be feeling. Convince yourself that you are sure to get this job. Be cheerful and quietly confident. Look alive and interested.

But, even if you do all this, you may of course still not get the job. This could be for one of several reasons – it does not mean that you are hopeless or underqualified (in fact, you may be overqualified). Your temperament may not be suited to the employer's, or the successful applicant may have got connections with the firm. Nowadays, it is a success to be seriously considered; only the lucky one gets the job.

Character

This is the most interesting part of a person, and is what makes him or her unique. Character is the combination of humour, honesty, ability to concentrate and many other virtues, or vices, which makes up a recognisable individual.

You do not have complete control of your character. Some characteristics were present at birth, and would have come out whatever the circumstances; others were taught you by your parents and upbringing. You may have perhaps noticed that certain characteristics seem to run in families, even though the individual members of that family also have their own personal characteristics.

After the age of five or six, however, you begin to see

the effect of your character on others. A very mean or aggressive child will quickly realise that people dislike his or her unpleasant characteristics and will probably change his or her behaviour accordingly.

Try to look for characteristics in yourself which irritate others, and consider whether there is anything you can do about them.

Intelligence

Intelligence is difficult to define. An approximate measurement can be gained with an IQ test (Intelligence Quotient test). The average IQ is 100, and most people fall between 90 and 110. The IQ test does not measure how you adapt to situations or how good your judgement is.

Introversion/Extroversion

An introvert is shy and feels ill at ease in large groups of people. An extrovert is more outgoing and makes friends easily.

Most people are somewhere in between. How introvert or extrovert you are will guide your choice of interests. If you enjoy stamp collecting or sewing, you are in some ways an introvert; if you like team sports and amateur theatricals you are more extrovert.

Shyness Almost all young people are shy, though some show it more than others. Shyness can be difficult to overcome. However, it helps if you are confident in your dress and appearance, and if you have a hobby or interest you can talk about. Shyness is largely a fear of being thought unattractive or uninteresting. Try to remember that everybody has good features, and has something interesting to say. It may well take time to overcome your shyness.

Sex appeal

It is very difficult to say exactly what it is that makes people sexually attractive. The marvellous thing is that everyone has qualities that make them attractive to someone.

Some people, call them lucky or unlucky — have faces or bodies that make them instantly sexually attractive. This cannot be explained scientifically. Such people often have to face more temptations and worries than the rest of us.

Remember that sex appeal is not everything. Other, more long-lasting qualities are much more important. Without them even the most attractive person soon becomes very dull.

RELATIONSHIPS (see FAMILY RELATIONSHIPS, p. 106, and SEXUAL RELATIONSHIPS, p. 118)

SCHOOL PROBLEMS

When you have left school, you may well look back to your time at school as one of the most complicated periods of your life. At school, you have to stick to a detailed timetable and share classes with up to 30 or 40 other pupils. There may be dozens of teachers and older pupils in authority over you. Away from school, you live a totally separate life, with family, relatives and friends. Often, you may find that your two lives do not seem to fit together very well. When things get tough, remember that if you can cope with school you can cope with anything!

Going to school

Few people enjoy going to school if, for example, they are having an examination that morning. It is only natural to feel a bit scared. Most days, however, going to school is simply part of the daily routine.

But some people feel scared every day — although this feeling often goes away once they are safely in school. The less confident they feel, the worse that worry can be. But it is important not to take the easy way out and stay away from school. Problems have to be faced up to, not run away from. It often helps to find a friend to go to school with.

At school
There will always be things about school that you do not like. It is simply not possible to get on well with every teacher and to be good at all lessons and activities.

School is intended to train you to be a useful adult by gaining qualifications and interests which will help you later on. If you are really miserable at school, it is far better to talk over the problems with your parents or a teacher you trust than to suffer silently. Most teachers, even if they hardly know you, will be sympathetic and helpful once they know the extent of your difficulties.

Bullies
There are three main types of bully. The first is the large boy or girl who cannot be bothered to fight someone of their own size, and so picks on weaker and smaller children. The second is the person who enjoys being boss, and bullies others to maintain their position. And the third, and most unpleasant, is the person who simply enjoys hurting people.

The only way to resist bullies is to stop them getting what they want. With some, silence and non-resistance is the best weapon; with others, friendship pacts against the bully may be the best answer. However, it is probably wisest to get the advice of an older person about how to deal with your particular problem. If you know that someone's life is being made unbearable by a bully, you should report this fact to a teacher.

SEXUAL RELATIONSHIPS

How do you know whether you should have sex with someone or not? Advertisements and the media give the impression that it is a natural part of any boy/girl relationship. Most people feel quite differently — and rightly so.

Sex is for couples who have formed a deep and mutual attachment. Without affection, sex is merely a form of physical release which in the end is emotionally unsatisfying. So do not have sex with someone unless you are absolutely sure you want to.

If you do not feel ready for sex, say so. Virginity is not something to be ashamed of. It is something to be given up to the right person, when you both feel ready. Not before! This applies to boys as well as girls.

Never force, shame or cajole a girl or boy to have sex. Sexual intercourse under the age of sixteen is illegal, and people can be harmed emotionally by having sex too young.

If you do decide to have sex, make sure you take proper contraceptive precautions. An unplanned and unwanted pregnancy is a disaster.

Promiscuity (frequent casual sex) cheapens the sexual act and can spoil things for when the right man or woman comes along. It also carries the risk of catching an unpleasant and possibly dangerous disease. Doctors now know that promiscuity from an early age increases the chances of a woman developing certain types of cancer.

Sex between people who are sure of their relationship is unlikely to be harmful, either physically or psychologically. But your religion and your moral beliefs are important, and must be taken into account when you decide whether or not to have sex. You should also consider the feelings of your family and friends, who may be shocked or hurt by your behaviour.

THE SUBCONSCIOUS

Everything you do, you do for a reason. For instance, you eat when you are hungry, and you drink when you are thirsty. Other actions do not have such obvious motives. You may go to the shops, not because you want to buy anything, but because you hope to meet a friend there. Sometimes this subconscious motive is easy to work out, at other times it is not so obvious. Your subconscious may even want to do something you think you do not want to do. Would you dive into a dangerous river to rescue a child without a second's thought? Only if the situation arose would you know the answer.

So the subconscious often guards its secrets. There are many books available to help you interpret the subconscious, but you will probably find that if you want to interpret your dreams in terms of sex, you will find that all your dreams are about sex, and if you want to interpret them in terms of motorbikes, they will be full of motorbikes!

Illness and the subconscious

If you have to do something you do not want to do, like going to school or to work, your subconscious may tell your body to feel ill. If your body obeys, you may get symptoms such as a headache, stomach ache or wheezing attack. You feel ill, and you are ill. But your illness is a sign of worry, rather than an actual disease.

If you are then allowed to stay at home, the subconscious has got what it wanted. And nobody, not even you, realises that you have brought on the illness yourself. So the subconscious tries the trick again and again so that your whole lifestyle may be affected. Once the illness is recognised as a sign of worry, the symptoms usually get less. This is because the subconscious realises there is no point in carrying on the trick.

6
Sex

FACTS ABOUT BOYS
The penis
The sex organs of a boy consist of a penis and two testicles. Most of the time, a boy's penis is soft, and is used only when he passes water.

However, when a boy is sexually excited, his penis enlarges, stiffens and points upwards. This is called an erection. This erection is caused by blood filling and engorging the boy's penis, enlarging it to about three times its normal size. Bone is not involved in keeping the penis erect. A boy is unable to pass water if his penis is erect.

Baby boys may get erections, but only after puberty (see p. 132) is a boy able to perform a mature sex act. Infant boys sometimes get into the habit of rubbing their erect penis, because even at that age the sensation is pleasurable.

The size or shape of the penis has no bearing on the amount of sexual pleasure it can give. There is no particular advantage in having a large penis.

A boy may notice that he has a number of small firm pale spots on the shaft of his penis. These are natural and are not a sign of disease. They are merely pimples on the sensitive skin of the penis.

The foreskin is a loose flap of skin which covers the head of the penis. It neither increases nor diminishes sexual sensations. It is often removed in an operation

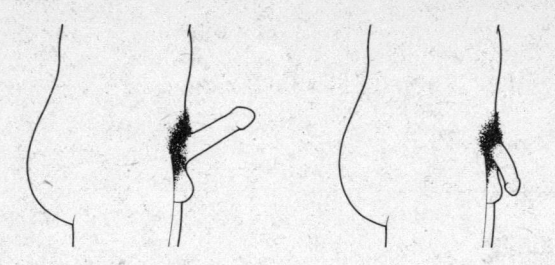

The penis, with and without an erection

called **circumcision**. This may be done for religious or hygienic reasons, fairly soon after the boy's birth. It may be needed later on if the child is getting infections in the tip of his penis.

The testicles

A boy has two testicles, both enclosed in a sack of skin called the scrotum. Before a boy is born, the testicles have dropped into the scrotum, having started off inside the body. On a cold day, a boy may notice that it is difficult to feel his testicles. They are pulled tight up into the top of the scrotum. This is quite natural.

But if a baby boy's testicles are not in the scrotum, it may be necessary to do a small operation to bring them down from above the scrotum.

The testicles produce a sex-fluid called semen which contains millions of sperm (tiny cells that swim in the sex-fluid, or semen). The testicles do not start to produce this fluid until the boy reaches puberty (see p. 132).

Pain in the testicles is always important, and a boy should never ignore it. You should see a doctor at once if you get pain for no obvious reason, or if the pain goes on longer than you expect after being hit in the testicles. This is because a testicle can twist within the scrotum. This is painful, and can be damaging unless corrected quickly by an operation.

Tight underwear will not cause permanent damage to the testicles. However it can keep them too warm

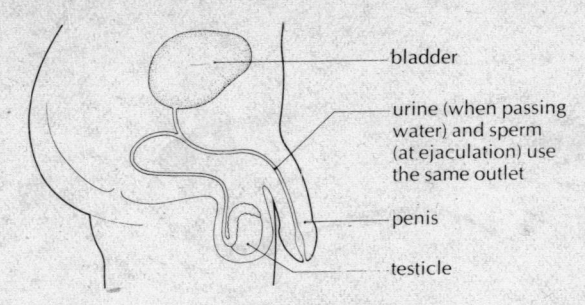

The genitals of a boy

and slow up the production of sperm. To remedy the situation, wear looser underwear!

Mumps before puberty cannot damage the testicles. After puberty, mumps cannot damage the testicles unless the boy gets a painful testicle infection called **orchitis**. Even with a bad attack, this almost never affects the testicles' ability to produce sperm. A doctor will be able to reassure you if you are worried.

A boy does not need two testicles. One is quite enough. It is not uncommon for a boy to lose one testicle because of an accident or because it became twisted. This will not affect his sex-life at all.

Ejaculation

When a boy is sexually excited, his penis becomes erect. If the erect penis is then rubbed, either during masturbation (see p. 133) or during sexual intercourse (see p. 135), the boy will experience pleasurable sensations.

After a few minutes (the actual length of time varies according to the individual, and according to the sexual excitement of the moment), the boy's penis ejaculates. This is a word to describe the moment of orgasm and the expulsion of a jet of semen from the penis. (An orgasm is an intensely pleasurable sensation which, for a few seconds, lifts a boy, or girl, into ecstasy.)

Many boys ejaculate during dreams at night. This is

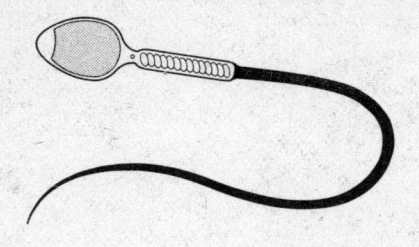

A sperm (magnified 300 times)

quite normal, although it tends to happen less often as the boy gets older. These dreams are often called 'wet dreams'.

Breasts

All boys have a small amount of breast. It is quite common for boys between twelve and sixteen to develop some swelling in the breast. This may be sufficient to become embarrassing, but there is no danger that they will continue to grow. It is merely a sign that the body hormones which are helping the rest of the body mature, are doing their job rather too well. There is no easy treatment and the swelling goes down after a few years.

FACTS ABOUT GIRLS

The vulva

The sex organs of the girl are hidden behind the folds of the vulva. But if she lies on her back and parts her legs, the folds of the vulva open out, and the hidden parts of her sex organs become visible.

At the front, normally only just hidden by the vulva, is the clitoris. Just behind that is the hole through which she passes water. This is called the urethra. And occupying the back half of the vulval opening is the entrance to the vagina.

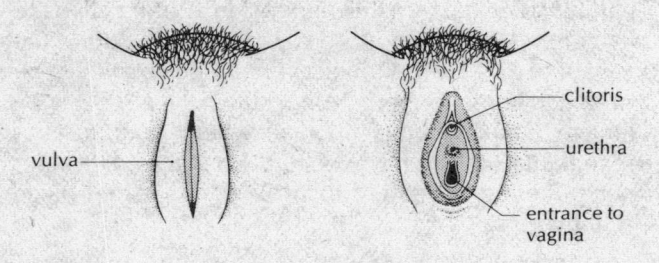

The genitals of a girl (viewed from below)

The clitoris
The clitoris is a small swelling which nestles between the folds of the labia near the front. This is the most sensitive part of a girl's sex organs. When she is sexually excited, it enlarges slightly.

The vagina
The entrance to the vagina is situated in the back half of the vulval opening. The vagina is an open sheath, big enough to accept the erect male penis. When a girl is sexually excited, the lining of the vagina becomes moist and well lubricated.

There is always some discharge from the vagina after puberty (see p. 132). The normal discharge is white, and may stain the underclothes. It is heaviest half-way between periods, at the time of ovulation (see p. 129). Some girls can actually tell the day that they ovulate by the increase in discharge. The flow also increases during pregnancy, with sexual excitement and whilst taking the contraceptive pill.

Regular washing and the use of talc will minimise any slight smell. Strong deodorants may irritate sensitive skin. Mild infections may lead to itching or soreness in the vagina and may cause the discharge to become smelly. These infections are not usually linked to sexual activity and are easily treated by a doctor.

In a young girl, the entrance to the vagina may be partially blocked by a thin flap of skin. This is called the hymen. If the hymen is there, only a small part of the vagina can be seen. However the hymen may well be stretched before puberty, especially if the girl is a keen athlete. If the hymen is still intact when the girl first has sexual intercourse, it will be torn when the boy's penis penetrates her. This may hurt a little and she may bleed slightly.

Breasts

The breasts, or mammary glands, consist of milk-producing tissue which is embedded in fat. They provide milk for the newborn baby, which he or she takes by sucking on the nipples. Most girls, whatever the size of their breasts, are able to produce sufficient milk to feed their baby, although sore nipples may make this difficult.

It is possible to have extra nipples on the chest lower down the body. They are usually very small and difficult to see.

Breast tenderness may occur just before a period starts. Prolonged breast tenderness can be an early sign of pregnancy, although this is obviously impossible if you have not had sex.

Breast size It is difficult for young girls to avoid comparing their own breast size with that of their friends. But a girl has no control over the size of her breasts, and neither exercise nor diets will alter their size. However, since the development of the breasts is under the control of a girl's sex-hormones, her breast size may vary during the monthly cycle. They may enlarge if the girl is on the contraceptive pill or if she is pregnant.

A girl may be shy of her growing breasts, but she should try to avoid walking in a hunched-up position in an attempt to hide them. It is quite common for a girl's breasts to be of different sizes; it does not mean that there is anything wrong.

It is important that a girl's bra should fit comfortably. The nipples are sensitive and may become sore in a badly-fitting bra.

Childbirth The flow of milk from the breasts starts fairly quickly after childbirth and usually continues for as long as the baby continues to breast-feed. If the baby is bottle fed, the breasts will be uncomfortable for a few days and then go back to normal once the milk production has stopped.

Some women are unable to breast feed because of difficulties with their breasts after giving birth. A baby will grow very well on bottled milk. However breast feeding is preferable to bottle feeding for several reasons. The natural milk is better for the baby and protects it from infections in the first few months of life. Many mothers find breast feeding enjoyable, but it does have its uncomfortable moments if the baby is a chewer, even though he or she has no teeth!

The internal sex organs

At the top of the vagina is the cervix. This feels like a smooth knob with a dent in it, and it is the entrance to the girl's womb (the uterus). The womb, usually about the size of a small orange sits on top of the vagina.

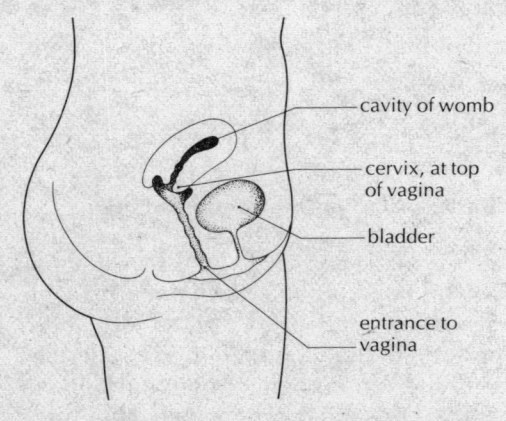

The internal sex organs of a girl (side view)

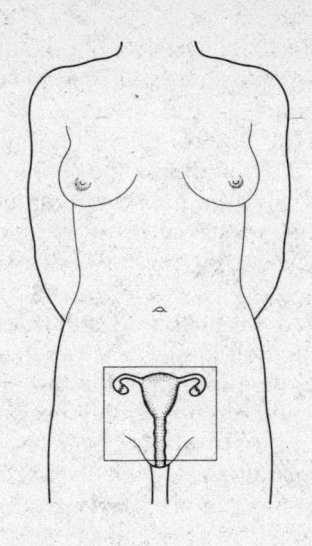

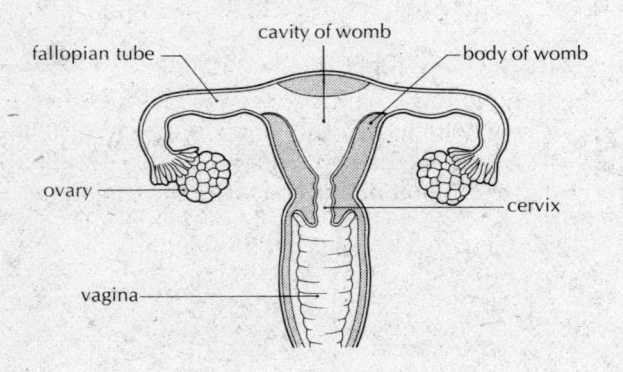

The internal sex organs of a girl (front view)

The womb is made of muscle with a small cavity in the centre. This is where the developing baby grows during pregnancy.

On either side of the womb are two ovaries. These are joined to the top corners of the womb by short, narrow tubes. These two tubes are called the fallopian tubes.

Menstruation
A girl becomes sexually aware at puberty (see p. 132), which occurs at any age between nine and sixteen. Her breasts and sexual parts grow, and her periods start.

The period A girl's period comes about every four weeks. It consists of bleeding which originates in the womb and passes out through the vagina. During each four-week cycle (or monthly cycle), the lining of the womb gradually thickens and becomes soft and spongy. At the end of the monthly cycle, the soft lining breaks up and flows out as period bleeding. This bleeding lasts for between 2 and 7 days. During this time, most girls use tampons or sanitary towels to absorb the blood.

Just before her period, a girl may feel moody and have headaches or stomach pains. These are an effect of female hormones. They usually wear off quite quickly.

The monthly cycle During the course of her monthly cycle, a girl produces a single egg from one of her ovaries. The egg takes about two weeks to mature, and is then released about half way between two periods. This releasing process is called **ovulation**.

The egg passes down the fallopian tube and into the womb. If sperm are present, either in the fallopian tube or in the womb, one sperm joins with the egg and fertilises it. The fertilised egg is sticky, and attaches itself to the soft, spongy lining of the womb. From this small beginning, a baby starts to grow.

If the egg does not meet a sperm, fertilisation cannot occur, and the egg dies. In this event, there is no need for further growth of the lining of the womb, so it is shed and the girl's period starts. If fertilisation does occur, and a baby starts to grow, the girl misses her period. If a normal period occurs, the girl cannot be pregnant.

Period problems
Period bleeding almost never causes anaemia (see p. 11). But if a girl regularly passes clots of blood during

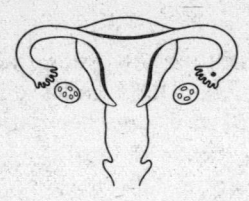

1. An egg is released from ovary (ovulation)

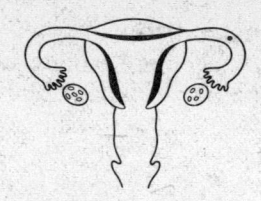

2. Lining of womb grows spongy and soft

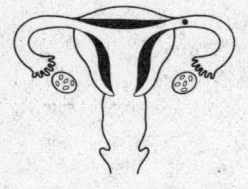

3. Egg, not fertilised by sperm, dies

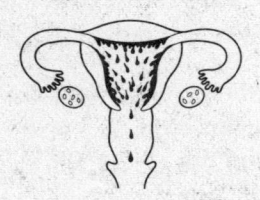

4. Spongy womb lining is shed (menstruation)

The menstrual cycle

her period, she should check with her doctor that all is well.

Most girls have a period about once a month, but it is not abnormal to vary from this pattern. However if a girl is on the contraceptive pill, her periods will be absolutely regular.

It is not unusual for a girl to miss her periods for a few months, especially if she is under some emotional strain. For instance, many girls miss periods when working for exams, when ill, or when leaving school. If there is any chance that her periods have stopped because she is pregnant, she should see a doctor.

If a girl's periods stop while she is on a diet, she should check with her doctor that the diet is not upsetting her hormones.

Premenstrual tension is the name given to a group of troublesome symptoms which may start a few days before a girl's period. They are caused by the female hormones. Stomach aches, breast discomfort, headaches and tiredness are all common; and if they are causing severe problems the girl should see a doctor. He or she will usually be able to suggest ways of reducing the symptoms. Premenstrual tension often lessens as the girl gets older, and may be helped by going on the contraceptive pill.

Pain on the first day of a period is common. It is caused by the womb muscles working to remove the menstrual blood. The pain always gets better once the period flow has started properly, and most girls find that aspirin or paracetamol taken regularly through that day helps lessen the pain.

HEALTH CHECKS
The breasts
Breast lumps are worrying because it is always possible that they may be caused by cancer. However, breast cancer is very uncommon in young people, and small soft lumps in the breast often occur around the time of the period.

Even so, girls should be aware of what their breasts feel like so that they can recognise any abnormality. Go to a doctor straight away if you have a lump that stays for more than a week, or that is hard and painful. Although it will almost certainly be nothing to worry about, it is best to make absolutely sure.

Breast cancer is a serious illness, and usually means having an operation for the breast to be removed. This is called a **mastectomy**. If the lump is small and completely removed, the disease is cured. Drug treatment and X-ray therapy (see p. 180) is also useful in treating breast cancer.

The cervix
The cervix (see p. 127) is situated at the top of the vagina.

All girls over the age of eighteen, and especially those who are sexually active, should have a smear test at regular intervals. The cervix is gently scraped, and the scrapings are then looked at under a microscope. It is an uncomfortable, but not a painful process.

The test detects changes in the cervix which indicate whether a cancer is *likely* to develop over the following ten years. This means that if the test is positive, a small operation can be done to prevent a very unpleasant disease. You should get advice from your doctor about how often the test should be done.

PUBERTY

Puberty is the word which describes the process of maturing sexually. Girls generally mature earlier than boys, but the age at which either sex matures is very variable. Most girls mature between the ages of nine and sixteen; most boys mature between eleven and sixteen. Some people become sexually mature outside these age ranges, and though this is unusual, it does not necessarily mean that anything is wrong.

Puberty is caused by a young body starting to produce sex hormones. In a boy, these sex hormones are produced in the testicles (see p. 122). In a girl, they are produced in the ovaries (see Menstruation, p. 129). The hormones are chemicals which circulate in the blood. The boys' hormones are different from the girls'.

In both boys and girls, the sex hormones cause the sex organs to develop and grow. A girl's periods start (see Menstruation, p. 129) and her breasts will develop. A boy becomes able to ejaculate (see p. 123).

The sex hormones also have other effects on the young person's body. At puberty, pubic hair around the genitals starts to grow. Later, more hair grows under the armpits. Boys grow a moustache and beard, and later develop hair on the chest. A boy's voice also changes at this time, becoming deeper, and eventually breaking.

SEXUAL ACTIVITY

Masturbation

Masturbation is the activity of fondling or rubbing the sex organs for pleasure. Even very young children masturbate, and at all ages both boys' and girls' sex organs are easily aroused. If rubbed, a boy's penis becomes erect, and a girl's clitoris becomes more prominent.

After puberty, masturbation usually results in orgasm (an orgasm is an explosive concentration of pleasure that marks the peak of the sex-act). A boy achieves orgasm by rhythmically rubbing his erect penis, sometimes concentrating on the sensitive tip. After a time, usually several minutes, he reaches orgasm and ejaculates.

A girl achieves orgasm by rhythmically stimulating her clitoris. This is done either by directly touching the clitoris, or by stroking inside the vagina, from where the sensations pass to the clitoris.

After boys have achieved ejaculation and orgasm, they generally need to rest for a time before they become sexually excited enough to repeat the experience. This may be a few minutes in a highly exciting situation, or as long as a few weeks if the boy has not any particular urge towards sexual activity. Wet dreams (see Ejaculation, p. 123) may replace masturbation as a form of sexual release.

After girls have achieved orgasm, they may feel sexually satisfied or else want to continue masturbating to achieve another orgasm.

Masturbation is not physically harmful in any way. It cannot damage the sex organs, and does not cause blindness, madness or any other illness.

How often people masturbate varies widely. Some people do it only very occasionally, while others do it several times a day.

Masturbation may provide a release for sexual energy which cannot be released in any other way. This is especially true in the first years of puberty. Later, as you begin to form close and loving relationships, masturbation becomes less important.

Kissing and petting

You will meet many people of the opposite sex that you feel attracted to. But you may not like some of them so much when you get to know them a little better. However, if you do feel attracted to someone whom you know and like, you will probably want to show your affection for them in a physical way. This is quite natural. And providing that you and your partner both feel the same way, it is a very enjoyable part of a relationship.

But, however enjoyable it is do not get carried away. Very heavy petting, in a state of partial undress, could result in pregnancy if the boy ejaculates near the girl's sex organs. Masturbation cannot lead to pregnancy provided that the boy's sperm is kept away from the girl's vagina.

When is it allowed to have sex?

This is a difficult question to answer because so much depends on the couple concerned. It is easier to say when a couple should not have sex.

Sexual intercourse is illegal under the age of sixteen.

Do not have sex if you are not taking contraceptive precautions (see p. 142). Any girl can become pregnant.

If you have religious, cultural or family beliefs that discourage sex before marriage, it is unwise to ignore them. Your action may have serious consequences later on.

If you are worried that you or your partner might have a sexually transmitted infection (see p. 147), do not have sex. Go to a doctor for a check-up.

If you have any doubts about your partner's commitment to your relationship, delay having sex. If someone is not emotionally prepared for sexual intercourse, it may affect them badly for a long time.

Only you can tell if you are ready to have sex with somebody. If the thought of it frightens you, or if you do not want to get emotionally involved with your partner, it is wrong to have sex.

Sex with a person you love is far more enjoyable than a casual encounter, or a one-night stand. Girls in particular react both physically and emotionally to their sexual partner and are likely to feel very hurt and bewildered by an early rejection.

HAVING SEX FOR THE FIRST TIME

It is a sad fact that many people lose their virginity almost by accident. In the heat of the moment, often during a good party, they suddenly decide to 'go the whole way'. In these circumstances, they often do not take contraceptive precautions. But remember, it is a complete myth that pregnancy cannot result from the first time of intercourse. It can – and frequently does!

The phsyical facts

During the sex act, the boy presses his erect penis against the entrance to the girl's vagina. The boy has usually felt the girl's sex organs with his fingers and is able to direct the head of the penis to the right spot. Often the girl helps by directing the boy's penis with her fingers.

The most usual position is for the couple to lie face to face, with the girl on her back (the so-called 'missionary' position). But this is not the only position; many couples find others more enjoyable. The advantage of the missionary position is that the erect penis rests comfortably, and at a natural angle, in the girl's vagina.

During intercourse, the couple may kiss and talk, and stroke each other's body. Certain areas of the body, called erogenous zones, are particularly sensitive. These include the nipples, the earlobes, the lips and the buttocks.

A girl who has not had intercourse before often has a

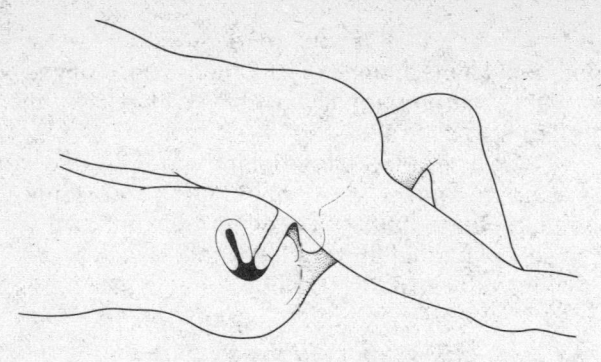

Intercourse – the boy's penis fits into the girl's vagina

fold of skin, called the hymen, protecting the entrance to the vagina. This may be torn or stretched during penetration by the penis. This is uncomfortable, and may cause slight bleeding, but the more gentle and understanding the boy is, the less discomfort there will be. This is because both the boy and girl will be relaxed and sexually excited, so allowing the natural lubricants of the penis and vagina to flow and help penetration.

A fully-grown girl is able to accept most boys without any difficulty. No physical damage will result from sexual intercourse, so long as force is not used by the boy during penetration.

Common difficulties

If neither partner has had sex before, both will be nervous. Anxiety in the boy may result in sexual over-excitement so that he ejaculates too soon or is so tense that he is unable to get an erection. Both occurrences, although they seem disastrous at the time, are very common. When the boy feels more at ease they are unlikely to take place.

If the girl is anxious, she too may become tense. Because she is not sexually excited, her vagina will not produce the flow of lubricant that makes penetration easy. It is then painful for both to try and have sex. A few minutes of affectionate relaxation, caressing and kissing one another, usually allows both partners to become aroused.

It is usually best not to hide the fact that you are having sex. Parents are surprisingly understanding, and most would prefer to be told than to find out from other people.

It is not sensible to have sex with lots of different partners. Sex is best if it is explored and perfected with one partner. The disadvantages of getting a reputation for 'sleeping around' are obvious. Those friends who want a stable, long-term relationship will be discouraged, and those interested only in the physical side of sex will be attracted to you. You also run the risk of picking up a sexually transmitted disease (see p. 147).

PREGNANCY
How does pregnancy begin
During sex, the boy ejaculates his sperm at the top of the girl's vagina. These sperm pass almost immediately through the narrow entrance at the top of the vagina, which leads to the womb. The sperm survive in the womb and the fallopian tubes for some days.

Ovulation occurs about two weeks before the girl's period is due to start (see Menstruation, p. 129). The egg is released from one of her ovaries and travels down the fallopian tube to the womb. It survives for about four days. If sperm are present, one sperm will meet the egg and join together in a process called fertilisation. They grow into a tiny developing baby, safely protected for the first few weeks in the soft lining of the womb. Because the baby is growing the lining does not become detached from the womb and the girl misses her period.

As the baby grows, it becomes surrounded by fluid. This is to protect it and to enable it to learn to move its arms and legs. After about five months, the mother can feel it moving and kicking. The baby gets food and oxygen from the blood which flows along the umbilical

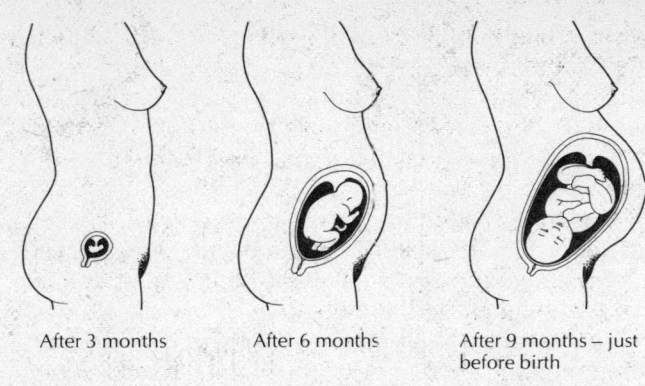

After 3 months   After 6 months   After 9 months – just before birth

Pregnancy

cord. This cord attaches the baby's navel to the lining of the mother's womb.

The developing baby

The baby grows very fast. In nine months, it grows from the size of a pinhead to about seven and a half pounds! The lower part of the abdomen begins to bulge about ten weeks after the missed period.

Every baby is precious and it is important that the mother takes proper care of it. For example, she should not smoke during pregnancy because smoking affects the baby's growth and may damage it in other ways. The nicotine in cigarettes cuts the supply of blood to the baby's growing brain. Similarly, she should have no more than the occasional alcoholic drink.

Having sex during pregnancy does no harm to the baby, nor is it affected by an vaginal infection (except possibly at the moment of birth). All drugs which a doctor recommends will be safe, but because of the effect on the baby, no unnecessary tablets should be taken.

How does a girl know she is pregnant?

The first sign of pregnancy is a missed period. There may of course be other reasons why a period may be late or missed (see Menstruation p. 129). But if the girl has had sex without contraceptive precautions in the previous three weeks, it is quite possible that her missed period is a sign of pregnancy.

The other signs that might show a girl is pregnant, become noticeable a few weeks later. Her breasts may become tender and slightly enlarged. The nipples may become brown. She will put on weight and she may well have early morning nausea or sickness.

If a period is two weeks overdue and the girl has reason to think she might be pregnant, she should have a **pregnancy test**.

Any doctor's surgery or any family planning clinic will be able to do the test. All the girl need do is provide a specimen of early morning urine. Some chemists and other agencies also advertise a pregnancy test service. Home pregnancy tests are often unreliable because the instructions have to be followed exactly and the slightest mistake can produce a false result.

Antenatal clinics

When a girl gets pregnant, she immediately becomes responsible for two lives – her own and her baby's. It is therefore very important that she books into an antenatal clinic as soon as possible, so that a doctor can keep a check on her health all through the pregnancy. He or she will also be able to advise the girl on what she can and cannot do, and make sure she is prepared for the birth, and for coping with a new baby.

Pregnancy nowadays is very safe, and it should also be happy. But a hidden pregnancy is unsafe – for both mother and baby – and often unhappy. A pregnant girl must be physically and practically prepared for the new arrival.

It is very difficult to tell your Mum that you are pregnant when you wish you were not, but it is far better to tell her than to let her find out.

Birth

Antenatal clinics make sure that the mother-to-be is physically and mentally prepared for the birth of her baby.

The expectant mother goes into labour some hours before the baby is born. The start of labour is often signalled by the 'breaking of the waters', which means that the fluid around the baby flows down from the womb out through the vagina.

Labour usually takes between six and ten hours. During this time the muscles in the womb push the baby downwards by squeezing for about thirty seconds at intervals of two to three minutes. These squeezes are called contractions. They are painful for the mother, and the midwife (a special nurse who is an expert on pregnancy) will give her painkillers if she wants them.

The entrance to the womb (the cervix), at the top of the vagina, slowly opens, and the baby comes head-first down the vagina. After the baby has been born, it is still attached by the umbilical cord to the lining of the

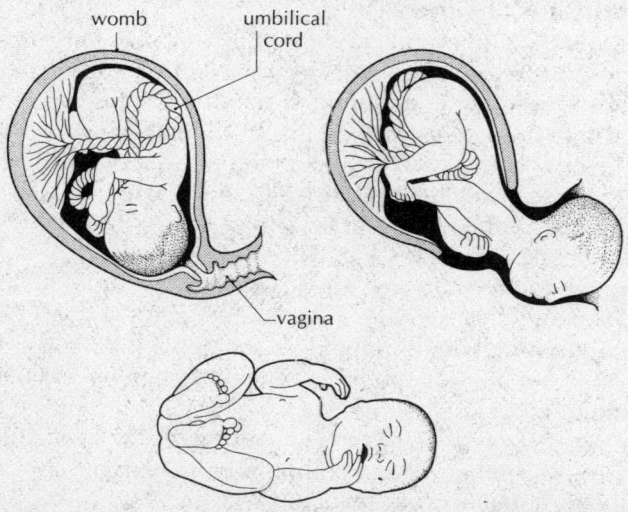

Birth – the umbilical cord from the baby's navel to the mother is cut after birth

womb. The midwife cuts and ties the cord. This does not hurt mother or baby. A few minutes later, the cord and its attachment to the womb comes away, and passes down the vagina and out. This is called the afterbirth.

Sometimes the baby's head does not pass out of the womb easily. When this happens, the doctor usually helps the mother-to-be with the birth. A metal instrument, called forceps, is used to protect the baby's head during the moment of birth.

Occasionally it is impossible for the baby to be born normally. It is then necessary to do an operation, called a Caesarian section. The mother is given anaesthetic and the baby is born through a cut in the lower part of her abdomen.

What can go wrong

Nowadays, pregnancy is very safe, provided that the mother-to-be attends antenatal clinics regularly and follows their advice. It is essential to attend a clinic because it is here that the girl's health is checked to ensure that all is well. Any problems are quickly spotted and dealt with. Tests are done to check that the baby is growing properly.

One pregnancy in ten ends in a **miscarriage**. This happens because Nature has decided that the pregnancy is not going right. It is a natural event which usually happens very early in the pregnancy. Despite old wives' tales, neither violent exercise, nor gin, nor hot baths will bring on a miscarriage.

Doctors may call a miscarriage by its medical term 'abortion'. Abortion in this sense is different from the operation to end pregnancy which is discussed on page 145.

No doctor can promise that a baby will be perfect. Sadly, a very few babies are born with heart defects or other problems. Most such problems are treatable, but unfortunately some are not. Luckily, all the worst problems are very uncommon.

CONTRACEPTION

If you and your partner decide to have sex, and do not want to start a family, it is very important that you take contraceptive precautions – always!

As it is girls who become pregnant, it is a fact of life that boys usually leave contraception to them. But boys should feel responsible too, and, if necessary, carry a supply of sheaths with them (see p. 144).

The contraceptive pill

The contraceptive pill stops a girl becoming pregnant by altering her hormone balance. It does this in a number of different ways, one of which is to block the cervix with mucus so that sperm cannot get into the womb to fertilise an egg.

This is the safest and best form of contraception for a girl who is having regular sex. But if she is having sex only occasionally, and she does not have a regular partner, it might be better for the boy to use a sheath (see p. 144). The girl will then not have to take powerful tablets, and will to some extent be protected from sexually transmitted diseases.

It is necessary to see a doctor to go on the pill. You can either see your family doctor or one at a family planning clinic (see p. 173). If you are healthy and the doctor feels you understand what you are doing, he or she will usually agree to prescribe the pill, even if you are under-age.

Being on the pill means that you must go to a clinic regularly. This is important because the pill does have side-effects and check-ups are needed. The clinic will tell your doctor you have been prescribed it unless there is very good reason not to. Your doctor will not discuss your health or treatment with anybody – not even your parents – without asking your permission.

Most girls are prescribed the combined pill. This needs to be taken every day for three weeks, followed by a week's break. It should be taken at about the same time every day. If one day's pill is missed, the contraceptive effect can be lost and another form of contraception should be used for the rest of the month. One or two pills are useless. A whole packet of pills must be taken on a daily basis.

Side-effects of the pill The pill is very safe. Even so, it is necessary for a doctor to check regularly on your weight and blood-pressure, both of which may increase slightly. Your periods may well become lighter and pre-menstrual symptoms may improve. Smoking is unwise.

Many girls who have just started on the pill feel a little sick or headachey for a month or so. This is usually not too distressing and the symptoms quickly disappear. However, a very few girls cannot tolerate the pill and are forced to find another form of contraception.

The coil

This is also known as the intra-uterine device (IUD). It is a good safe method of contraception.

There are several different types of coil, but they all consist of a small piece of plastic with a cotton thread attached to it. Some have a thread of copper wire round them to improve their efficiency.

Before a coil is inserted into the womb your doctor will examine you internally. This will not hurt. Then the coil is threaded into a plastic straw and passed into the vagina and inside the womb. The straw is then withdrawn leaving the coil in place. It is an uncomfortable, but not painful procedure. The coil stays in place, unnoticed, until it is removed by pulling on the cotton thread. Neither thread nor coil get in the way of sex at all.

Disadvantages The womb is fairly small before it is stretched by pregnancy. For this reason, some girls who have never been pregnant find that the coil is painful. It is often not the best method of contraception for young girls.

The presence of a coil in your womb may add about one day to the length of your period. The coil's other disadvantage is that it can make gonorrhoea (see p. 148) and other infections worse. It is not quite as safe a method as being on the pill, but it does have the advantage that you can just forget about contraception until the next check-up from the doctor.

The cap or diaphragm

Girls are fitted with a cap at a family planning clinic. A doctor examines you to find out what size cap you need and a nurse then teaches you how to insert it. The cap is very safe if used properly. It consists of a circle of flexible wire which supports a thin rubber dome. Sperm-killing cream is spread on either side of the dome, which is then inserted into the vagina so that it covers the entrance of the womb. It is very important that the cervix is covered.

Although it is a bit of a nuisance to put in in a hurry, it is very safe. It is an excellent method for a girl who is well-organised. But if you are the type of girl who is always losing things and who acts on the spur of the moment, another method would be safer.

The sheath

This is otherwise known as the condom or french letter. If used correctly, it is an excellent method of birth control.

The boy fits a thin rubber sheath onto his erect penis, using sperm-killing cream to act as a lubricant. This prevents the sperm from reaching the vagina. After intercourse, he removes the sheath, taking care not to spill the sperm.

Withdrawal method

The withdrawal method involves the boy withdrawing his penis from the girl's vagina before he ejaculates. It does not work! If a boy is sexually excited a small amount of sperm may leak from his erect penis even before ejaculation. Even if he only puts his penis near the girl's vagina, hardly penetrating her, she can become pregnant. (Human nature being what it is, there is even more of a risk, if he should lose control and finish what has been started!)

Douches
Washing out the vagina after intercourse is a waste of time. The sperm enter the womb within seconds of ejaculation, and by the time a douche has been used, it is already too late.

Rhythm method
The rhythm method involves calculating the time in a girl's monthly cycle when pregnancy is possible, and not having intercourse at that time. It is a highly unreliable method and is only useful for older couples, particularly Roman Catholics whose religion forbids them any other method.

Pregnancy is possible for approximately 4 days either side of ovulation (see p. 129), and ovulation occurs a set number of days (usually 14) *before* the next period begins. However, a young girl's periods are often irregular, thus making it almost impossible to calculate the 'safe' time for sexual intercourse. Even the fact of having sex can alter the day on which her period will come. Thus, since the rhythm method relies on accurate forecasting it is extremely risky for young people to rely on this method of birth control.

ABORTION

Abortion is the medical term used by doctors to describe both a miscarriage (see p. 141) and the operation done to stop a pregnancy. Some people have an abortion operation because having a baby would present too much of a risk to their health. More commonly, abortion operations are performed on girls and women who have become pregnant by mistake and who do not want to have their baby.

If you find that you are unexpectedly pregnant, you will probably be very scared. You will probably be nervous of telling your parents, and perhaps even your boyfriend. You may feel unable to cope with the enormous changes in your life a baby would bring. But no matter how scared you are, do not try to hide your pregnancy and on no account try to make yourself miscarry. You will not succeed and you will be risking your life. The infection and heavy bleeding that this can cause are both very dangerous in early pregnancy.

Do not hurry into the decision to ask for an abortion. Talk over the situation with your parents and boyfriend. You will probably find that your parents in particular are much more sympathetic and understanding than you thought possible. With their help and advice, you may well find that your attitude changes. You may find that you want to have the child, when your emotional feelings sort themselves out.

If, when the child is born, it becomes impossible to look after it properly, adoption can be arranged. There are many loving couples who are not able to have children and who would make excellent parents. Alternatively, your parents, or other relatives, may be able to help care for it.

However, if after discussing all the alternatives, you still feel it would be best to have an abortion, no time must be lost. The operation is best done within six weeks, and no later than fourteen weeks, of missing your period. The abortion is usually arranged through your doctor who, if he or she agrees to the operation, will arrange your admission to a hospital or nursing home. If not, there are agencies and organisations in most large towns that will be able to help (see p. 181).

The abortion is done in hospital under general anaesthetic. It is usually only necessary to stay in hospital for a few hours, but like all operations there are risks. Bleeding and infections can occur. To lessen the chances of this happening, it is very important that you rest with your family or friends for several days afterwards.

Even if you really want an abortion, do not feel surprised if you feel very upset after the operation. This is quite natural. You will need a lot of understanding from your family and friends. And on no account must you risk getting pregnant again too soon. It takes time to get over the effects of the operation, so you must either avoid sex or use a reliable form of contraception.

SEXUALLY TRANSMITTED DISEASES

Sexually transmitted diseases (or venereal diseases) are diseases which are spread by sexual contact or acts of great intimacy. Obviously if neither partner has had sex with anyone else, or if neither partner has got a venereal disease, neither can catch it from the other. STD cannot be caught from lavatory seats, from towels, from bedding or from clothes.

Common symptoms

The symptoms of sexually transmitted disease are the same as those caused by some other infections. These other infections are less severe, but they do need treatment from a doctor. In either case, boys may notice a burning pain in the penis when urinating; pus or a bloody discharge from the tip of the penis or from the anus; sores on the penis, which may or may not be painful. Girls may notice a burning pain when urinating (this also commonly happens with urinary infections), a smelly discharge from the vagina or sores around the vulva, which may or may not be painful. Girls are particularly likely to have infections without noticing them.

The best way of making sure you do not catch one of these diseases is not to have sex with someone who sleeps around. But if you are determined to go ahead, a sheath should be used. It will give at least some protection from diseases of this sort.

All these diseases are curable. But it is important that treatment is given as early as possible. Otherwise they may eventually cause serious trouble.

A doctor will be quite happy to see and reassure you if you are not sure about any symptoms you might have. Anything you tell him is absolutely confidential. If you do not want to see your own doctor, go to a special clinic (see p. 174).

What are the diseases?

Gonorrhoea This is a common sexually transmitted disease. It is because of gonorrhoea that those who sleep around should take particular care. It is important that if you notice any of the symptoms described above, or if you are worried that your partner might have it, you go to a doctor for a check-up. The disease can cause serious trouble later if it is not treated immediately. Luckily it is easily dealt with by a doctor. Do not attempt to treat this yourself. Some antibiotics clear up the symptoms without killing the disease. It is important to have the right antibiotic.

Syphilis The first symptom is a painless sore on the penis or vulva. A few weeks later, the glands swell, a rash develops and the patient feels ill. If left untreated, the disease can progress over many years to untreatable heart trouble and even madness. It occurs mainly in homosexuals. All pregnant girls are checked with a simple blood test for the disease as it can harm unborn babies.

Urethritis This is a troublesome but not dangerous infection which affects the urethra, the tube from which you pass water. The infection is also known as honeymoon cystitis, or NSU (Non-specific urethritis).

Vaginal infections Despite popular belief, these are not usually sexually transmitted and are very common. Thrush, monilia, candida (which are all the same thing) and trichoma, are mild infections which cause a discharge from the vagina and often some soreness. They are all easily treated by your family doctor. Do not be embarrassed to go to him. These infections are not 'dirty' or dangerous.

Other diseases All these diseases should be treated by a doctor:

AIDS is a disease which occurs mainly in homosexuals who have many partners. It is probably caused by an infectious virus which destroys the body's ability to defend itself against infection – thus its name the *Acquired Immune Deficiency Syndrome*. Modern medical science can keep the patient alive for a time but the disease itself is untreatable. Fortunately it is very rare at present.

Genital warts Unlike ordinary warts, these do not get better, and should be treated early before they spread.

Herpes A troublesome and painful infection which causes blistering around the sex organs.

Pubic lice These are little insects which live in the pubic hair. They are itchy and easy to detect.

THE DEVELOPMENT OF SEXUALITY

Your sexual development in a physical sense is a development over which you have no control. Your body hormones do all the work.

Your understanding about sex, and what you want from sex, develops in a rather different way and depends on your family, your friends and your background. Imagine you have a blackboard in your mind. On that blackboard there is one heading – Sex. At birth, the rest of your board is empty. From then on, the details of every sex experience you have is written on the board. Important experiences are written large; other, less significant experiences are only lightly chalked in. As you grow up, the board gets filled with writing. Some of your sexual experiments will have been fun, others less so; some of the experiments will have been alone, some with a friend, and some, perhaps, with a group of friends.

But despite the variety of experiences, most people who are growing out of adolescence can look at their imaginary board and say, 'I've read, talked and experimented quite a lot with sex, and I now know what I want. I want a loving boyfriend, or girlfriend (depending on whether it is a girl or boy speaking) and I want a good sex life and happy family life with him, or her, when we marry.'

But not everyone will come to this conclusion when they read their imaginary board. A very few people, for example, will have had an upsetting experience when young which is written in red right across their board. Because of it they might decide never to have anything to do with sex again. This is one reason why children should never be subjected to frightening sexual experiences.

Pornography can also affect the way people regard sex, particularly if they come into contact with it when young. For this reason, it should be kept away from all children.

HOMOSEXUALITY

A homosexual is a person who is attracted to someone of the same sex and wants sexual contact with him or her. Female homosexuals are often called lesbians.

People make jokes about poofs or queers, but many homosexuals are sensitive and cultivated people who reveal their sexual preferences only to others of the same inclinations. They are often not noticeably different from anyone else.

Many homosexuals are capable of loving people of the opposite sex and form so-called heterosexual relationships. These people are bisexual, i.e they can love and enjoy loving both male and female partners. Most bisexuals have a homosexual or heterosexual preference.

It is illegal to have homosexual contact with a boy under the age of twenty-one.

Crushes

At puberty (see p. 132), many young people develop a strong attraction towards someone of the same sex. The object of their admiration is often an older person. Feelings of this sort are quite normal and should not necessarily be taken as a sign of homosexuality. The will almost certainly disappear once the boy or girl develops an interest in the opposite sex.

APPROACHES FROM STRANGERS

Some young people are approached by adults for sexual reasons. It is often unpleasant and frightening. If you are accosted, or if you see a young child being accosted, you should tell your parents and make sure that the police are informed.

Always be on guard against strangers. Be careful, too, not to sexually tease an adult. Sexually experienced adults may misinterpret your intentions. Remember that as a young person you are sexually attractive. Only direct your sexuality at those you like and feel attracted to.

7
Serious Illnesses

This section is about some of the more common illnesses and diseases which *may* determine how long someone can expect to live, or how active they are. Most of them affect people who are middle-aged or older.

They include diseases which, although they can be helped, cannot be completely cured. Sufferers usually know that they will never be as fit as they were in their younger days. However, they must keep active and not let themselves become invalids unnecessarily. Being told that you have high blood pressure or heart trouble is not a death sentence; it is a reason for enjoying life more and worrying less about work and money.

People are living longer nowadays and so the body is expected to do more. Not surprisingly, parts of the body begin to show signs of wear and tear after a time. It is largely a matter of luck which part gives trouble first. Compare the body to a bicycle. If the ball-bearings go, you might get arthritis; if the chain goes, you may get heart trouble, and so on.

We all have to die sometime, and something has to cause our deaths. However, most people want to live as long as they can, and many health problems can be delayed, or even avoided altogether, if you look after your body when young. This means not smoking, keeping to a sensible diet and having enough exercise. Do these three things and you will have a better chance of a long and vigorous life.

ARTERY DISEASE

None of us can avoid artery disease as we get older, although some people are more prone to it than others. Many people get no trouble at all.

Your arteries carry blood from the heart to every part of the body (see CIRCULATION, p. 20). These arteries gradually silt up, like the inside of a kettle, so that if you were to live until you were 200 years old, your blood would hardly flow at all. You cannot avoid this process affecting your arteries.

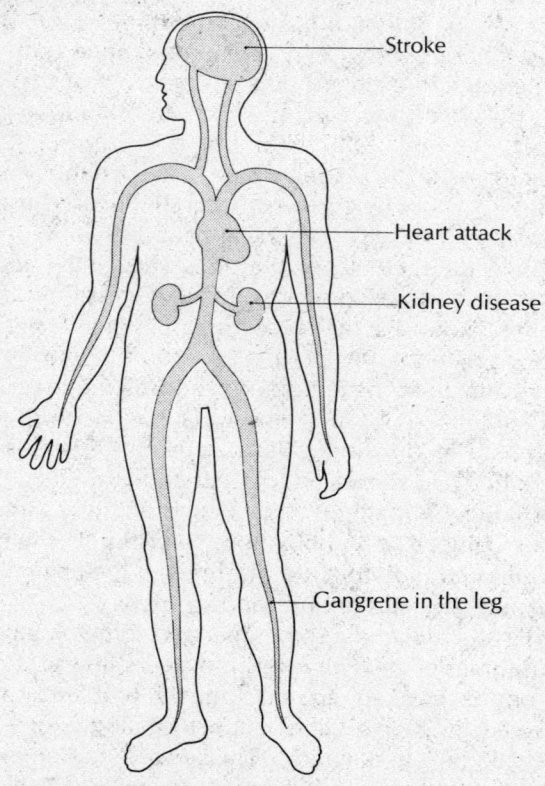

Artery disease can affect any part of the body. It may cause any of these conditions

Of course, we are all long dead before we are 200 years old. But if one artery becomes blocked especially quickly, that part of the body will die from a lack of life-giving, oxygen-carrying blood.

A blocked artery in the heart causes a heart attack (also known as a thombosis or coronary); a blocked artery in the brain causes a stroke (see BRAIN DISEASES, p. 158). Arteries may become blocked anywhere in the body, and the damage that results depends on where the artery is, and how big it is.

Artery disease is made worse by smoking, and is helped by taking regular exercise and eating sensible food. But the amount that it affects people varies. It is largely a matter of luck whether artery disease runs in your family or not.

ARTHRITIS (see also p. 13)

Arthritis causes pain in the joints, and there are many different types of arthritic pain.

Gout

Gout is very painful. It often attacks the big toe. There is usually no obvious reason why it has started, though it can run in families. With modern treatment, it is not usually a troublesome disease.

Osteoarthritis

As people get older, their joints do not work quite as smoothly as they once did. Your granny will never run like a two-year-old again! Her stiff and painful joints are affected by osteoarthritis — a complicated word meaning that they have been damaged by wear and tear through the years.

Tablets help considerably to relieve the pain and stiffness. But little can be done for the swelling that affects the hands and feet in particular. If a hip is giving a lot of pain, the sufferer may be offered a hip replacement operation. This remarkable treatment enables crippled old people to walk again without pain, and is usually well worth the risk of a major operation.

Other types of arthritis
Rheumatoid arthritis mainly affects the joints, but other similar types mainly attack the skin, the bowels or the heart.

All these types of arthritis are treatable, though many are incurable. However, they may improve of their own accord. The doctor's job is to control the symptoms until the disease gets better on its own. Luckily, there are very strong and efficient drugs available to treat all types of arthritis.

BLOOD DISEASES

Blood poisoning
Blood poisoning is dangerous, but does not occur very often now that modern antibiotics can be used to kill the bacteria germs which cause the infection. Before antibiotics were invented, many people died of blood poisoning. Wounded soldiers, and women who had just given birth, were particularly likely to die from it.

Leukaemia
Leukaemia is a type of blood cancer (see p. 159). It is very difficult to say anything very definite about it because there are so many different varieties. However, all varieties have been cured, and with some the chances of a complete cure are good. The development of modern treatments means that the chances are improving all the time. The treatment, which includes strong drugs and sometimes X-ray therapy (see p. 180), is not pleasant and makes the patient feel ill and miserable, but it is worth the effort.

Sickle cell disease
Sickle cell disease mainly affects West Indians and black people of African origin.

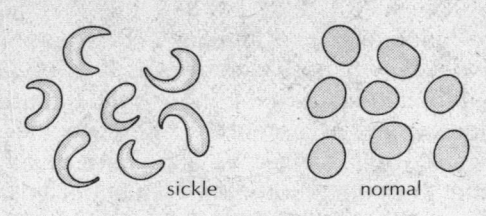

Normal blood cells can take on a sickle shape if you have sickle cell disease

Everybody's blood is made up of a colourless fluid, which has millions of tiny red cells floating in it. These red cells carry oxygen to all parts of the body. But if a person has sickle cell disease these cells tend to stretch out into a useless 'sickle' or banana shape and so cannot carry oxygen properly. They also block the small blood vessels. This causes pain and often needs treatment in hospital.

If you have sickle cell trait, your blood cells are quite normal. The only disadvantage is that if you marry someone who also has sickle cell trait and you have a child, your child may have sickle cell disease. Anybody can ask for a simple blood test which will detect whether or not he or she has sickle cell trait.

The advantage of having sickle cell trait is that you are partially protected against severe types of malaria (see p. 57).

BLOOD PRESSURE TROUBLE

Your doctor can easily measure the pressure of blood in your arteries (see CIRCULATION, p. 20). He or she winds an inflatable piece of material round your arm, and measures the pressure needed (or the amount he or she has to squeeze) to block the blood circulation to the arm.

High blood pressure (hypertension)
Most people have a normal blood pressure, but as they get older, their blood pressure may go up. High blood

pressure tends to run in families and is particularly likely to develop in those who smoke.

High blood pressure does not usually cause any noticeable symptoms, except during pregnancy. In this case, it can be quite dangerous, although it usually gets better after the child is born. But if left untreated, it can be dangerous for both mother and child. People with high blood pressure may get heart trouble (see p. 163) or artery diseases at a young age (see p. 154). They should get advice from a doctor about how much exercise to take. High blood pressure is usually easily dealt with by taking special tablets. Apart from pregnant women with high blood pressure, who need plenty of rest, it is not usually necessary to take things easy. Nobody dies from high blood pressure alone.

Anybody over the age of thirty-five should have their blood pressure checked every five years or so. Girls who are pregnant, or who are on the contraceptive pill, also need to have their blood pressure checked regularly.

BRAIN DISEASES (see also OLD AGE, p. 114)

Strokes

A stroke occurs when an artery in the brain becomes blocked (see ARTERY DISEASE, p. 154). This blockage, sometimes called a thrombosis, damages the brain, so that part of it does not work. Strokes almost always affect old people.

Because the brain is damaged, part of the body is often paralysed. How well a stroke victim recovers depends on many things, but the more they try to get better, the more likely they are to improve.

A stroke is a very frightening experience, and is also embarrassing if it leaves the person unable to drink without dribbling, or unable to go to the lavatory without asking for help. Never forget that somebody who has had a stroke is still a thinking man or woman who is trying to relearn how to control their muscles and limbs. However bad the stroke, they need to be treated as an intelligent adult.

Multiple sclerosis (MS)
This is a progressive disease which inactivates nerves around the body, causing paralysis and numbness. But although it is incurable, it develops slowly and is helped by modern treatments. In fact, well over half of those who develop MS are not even slightly disabled as much as five years later and can look foward to the future with confidence. People who do become disabled can, with determination, still lead active lives, despite the difficulties.

Parkinson's disease
This is an upsetting illness because people who contract it can think perfectly well, but cannot make their body do what they want it to do. It particularly affects the fingers and face muscles. This means, for example, that it becomes difficult to smile and almost impossible to do up buttons. Often, being unable to smile means that other people are less friendly. The condition is helped with tablets, but is not curable.

CANCER

There are as many different types of cancer as there are parts of the body. A cancer starts when part of the body tissue suddenly starts to grow uncontrollably. This growth presses on the other parts of the body and damages them.

Breast cancer
For information about lumps in the breast, see p. 131.

Chances of recovery
Nobody knows why cancers start, but doctors do know quite a lot about how they develop (see TOBACCO, p. 102). There are treatments for almost all cancers, but

the chances of success vary enormously with the type of cancer, and how long it has been growing.

It is always difficult to predict which cancers are curable and which are not. Anyone with cancer of the skin, the large bowel or the womb usually has an excellent chance of a complete cure. Early cancers of the breast, of the bone and most glands also have a good chance of a complete cure.

Cancers of the lung, stomach and ovary are less easily treated.

But it must be stressed that these guidelines are very approximate. There are types of lung and other more serious cancers that are completely curable. Only a doctor can give the facts about an individual, and his or her particular cancer.

Treatment

It is essential that treatment should be started as early as possible. If you have any worrying symptoms, go to your doctor straight away. It is extremely unlikely that anything serious will be wrong, but it is best to be on the safe side.

Cancers can be treated in three different ways: a surgical operation can be done to remove the growth; drugs can be given to destroy the cancer; or X-ray therapy (see p. 180) can be given to shrivel up the cancerous growth.

None of these treatments are pleasant, and all of them make the patient feel quite ill while the treatment is going on. Sometimes more than one type of treatment is needed.

COLITIS

Colitis is the name given to bowel upsets which cause diarrhoea (see p. 27) and stomach pains for weeks on end. It is worse than an ordinary bug which causes diarrhoea and vomiting because it goes on for so long.

It is very unpleasant to have to worry all the time where the nearest lavatory is! There is often no obvious cause.

Colitis caused by infection
Colitis is commonly caused by an infection which produces symptoms of diarrhoea for some weeks. It is particularly likely in tropical countries. Treatment is usually simple once the cause of the infection is known.

Other types of colitis
Ulcerative colitis, **Crohn's disease** and the **irritable bowel syndrome** affect people in different ways. Some people have only one attack whereas others suffer for long periods. Modern treatments are very effective, but as yet there is no certain cure for any of these types of colitis.

GALLSTONES

If you press hard under your ribs on your right-hand side, you will be pressing against your liver. Hanging down from the liver is the gall-bladder, which is full of digestive juices waiting to flow when you eat your next meal. Occasionally, these juices form crystals (in the same way that sugar or salt solutions sometimes do), and these crystals are called gallstones.

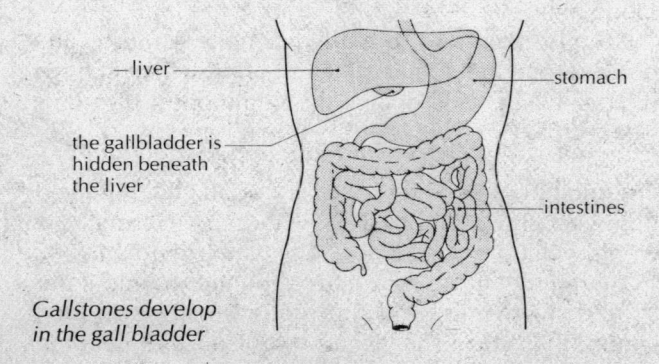

Gallstones develop in the gall bladder

Gallstones are very common in older people and many have them without knowing. But they can cause problems, such as severe stomach ache and yellow jaundice (see p. 42), which make an operation necessary. This is a very safe, but still quite major operation. The patient can therefore expect to stay in hospital for at least ten days, and will not be able to go back to heavy work in under three months.

GLAND PROBLEMS

A gland is any organ in the body which produces a fluid. The fluids may be released onto the skin (e.g. sweat) into the bowel (e.g. digestive juices) or into the blood. These last are called hormones.

Hormones

Hormones circulating in the blood not only affect how energetic, how sleepy, how sexy or how frightened you feel, but also physical things like how much you urinate and how much you sweat.

Doctors sometimes give their patients tablets to increase the natural hormones in the body, or to make the hormone glands work faster or slower. Any of these treatments affect the amount of normal hormones in the body. The contraceptive pill (see CONTRACEPTION, p. 142) and steroids (see p. 101) are both hormone pills.

Because there are so many hormone glands in the body, there are many different things that can go wrong. Diabetes is one of the commonest disorders (see p. 26).

Thyroid hormone The thyroid is a small gland situated in the neck just in front of the windpipe. Normally, it works well producing a hormone called thyroxin.

Thyroxin controls how active you are feeling. If the thyroid overworks, you run around, using so much energy that you soon exhaust yourself and become

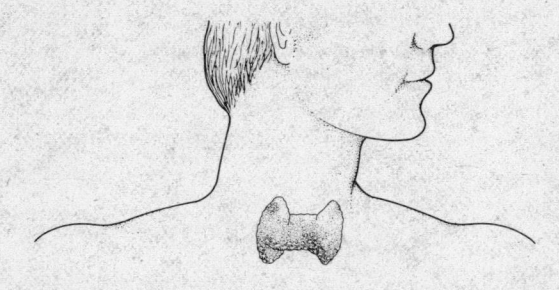

Your thyroid gland is in front of your windpipe near the bottom of your neck

quite thin. If the thyroid is not producing enough thyroxin, you will slow up mentally, and become sleepy and fat.

Both these problems are easily treated by a doctor. But of course most sleepy, fat people are sleepy and fat because that is just what they are like, as are most thin, very active people.

HEART TROUBLE

There are two types of heart trouble. First, there is heart trouble you are born with, such as a 'hole in the heart'. And second, there is heart trouble which comes on as you get older.

Heart trouble you are born with

The heart is a complicated pump rather like a double bicycle pump, but it is made of soft muscle, rather than plastic and metal. Usually the heart develops perfectly when a baby is in its mother's womb. But occasionally something goes wrong and there is a defect in the heart's structure.

Sometimes – luckily not very often – the defect is so bad that the new baby does not live after birth. More often, the defect is only discovered when a doctor

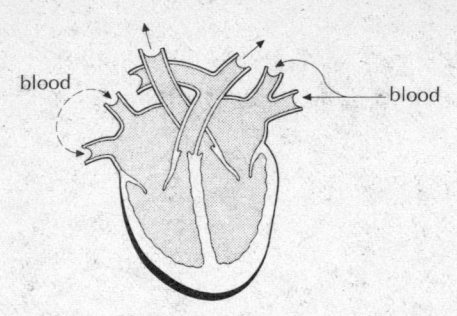

The complicated way that the normal heart works

listens to the baby's heart. Fortunately, most such defects right themselves as the baby grows older, although some children need special tests and an operation to get better.

A 'hole in the heart' does not mean that blood is leaking out of the heart. It simply means that there is a small leak between the compartments of the pumping heart. Imagine a bicycle pump with a small hole in the piston. If the hole is too large, the pump will not work at all. But if the hole is small, you just have to pump a little bit harder.

A hole in the heart can be repaired with an operation, but most holes are small and need no treatment.

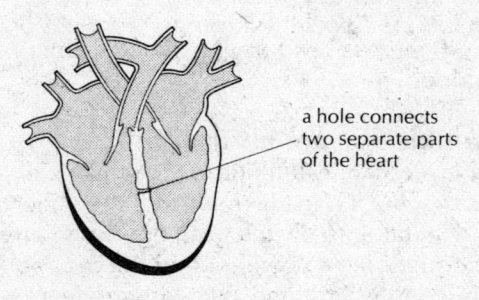

A hole in the heart

Heart trouble in later life

Almost all heart trouble is caused by artery disease (see p. 154). Just as the hand needs an artery to supply it arteries are needed to provide energy-rich blood to keep the heart pumping

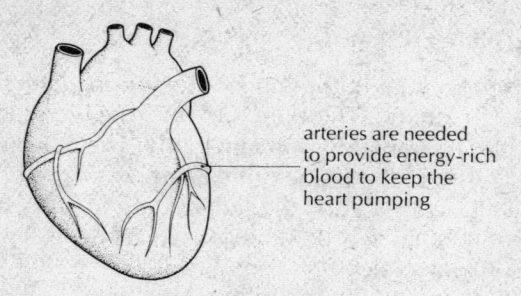

The heart needs its own blood supply

with life-giving blood, so the heart muscle needs arteries to supply it. In fact, the heart needs a large supply of blood, because it is working hard all the time.

Angina This is the medical word for a pain in the chest caused by strain on the heart. There are lots of other reasons for chest pains. You have probably had pains from indigestion or from a 'stitch' yourself. Angina is more serious and should be taken as a warning not to overwork and strain the heart. It is not the same as a heart attack (see below). The pains can be helped by treatment from a doctor.

Heart attack If one of the main arteries, which supplies the heart muscle with blood, is blocked, a small section of the heart muscle dies. The result is a heart attack (also called a thrombosis or coronary). A small heart attack is not too serious, and the patient can recover in a month or so. But obviously a large heart attack can be quite dangerous, and can even stop the heart working altogether.

Heart failure Quite a number of old people suffer from heart failure. The heart of a person who has lived for seventy years or so will have pumped over 200 million times! Not surprisingly the heart valves become rather leaky and the heart muscle becomes a bit soft. Because the heart is not pumping as well as it used to, fluid collects in the ankles, making them puffy, and it becomes difficult to breathe normally. Doctors can usually treat this trouble fairly easily with tablets.

KIDNEY DISEASE

The kidneys are tucked under the ribs on either side of your back bone. Their job is to filter the blood, cleaning it as it circulates round the body. The poisons they filter off from the blood are passed out of the body in urine. Like the heart, the kidneys are at work all the time (although they do slow down at night to let you get a good night's sleep).

Kidney failure

The kidneys of old people often do not work as well as they once did because they are wearing out. Nothing can be done about this.

Kidney failure in the young is a different problem altogether. There are many different types of kidney disease that can affect them. Some have only a short-lasting effect on the working of the kidneys, and the person quickly recovers. Others damage the kidneys so seriously that that they can never be repaired.

Somebody with very badly damaged kidneys would die within days if they did not have treatment. There are two types of treatment, both of which are very expensive.

A **kidney machine** does the job of the kidneys by filtering the patient's blood as it circulates through the machine. This needs to be done for several hours at a time, at least three times a week. Each machine costs as much as a large house to buy, and nearly as much as that to run a year.

A **kidney transplant** is a marvellous operation, which is truly life-saving. A kidney from a healthy donor is transplanted into a patient. It is very important that the new kidney matches the one that is removed. Many special tests are done to ensure a good match. Anybody who has seen someone cured by this operation will want to carry a kidney donor card.

Kidney donor cards are available at any health centre or hospital clinic. Once the card is filled in, it is proof that you have thought about transplants and would be happy to give your kidneys to an ill person after your death.

It should be stressed that there is absolutely no chance that the kidneys will be removed while you are still alive. It is now possible to be 100 per cent sure that a person is dead, even if their heart is kept going by a machine.

PHYSICAL HANDICAP

A physical handicap may be merely inconvenient (as with a weak arm for example) or a disastrous and crippling disability (such as would occur after a badly broken neck).

If the neck or back is broken and the spinal cord damaged, the body is paralysed below the level of the break. The indignity of needing help all the time, and the consequent feeling of helplessness can be very depressing. This is especially true in the first few months after such an injury.

If you meet someone with a handicap, remember their feelings. They are often clever and should never be treated as idiots. Help should be offered casually but only if it is needed, and carried out without fuss. Do not do more than you need. Do not worry if they are a bit sensitive. In the same situation, you probably would be too.

Spina Bifida

Children who are severely handicapped from birth and confined to wheelchairs, are often victims of spina bifida. This is a deformity of the spine which blocks the nerves of the spinal cord, thus causing paralysis. They may be mentally handicapped as well.

Other handicaps

Less serious handicaps are still frustrating and embarrassing. A severe limp can be caused by a hip dislocated at birth, by having one leg weaker or shorter than the other, or by a severe bend in the backbone. A weak arm or leg is usually caused by damage occurring at birth. These limbs deformities and weaknesses are not inherited by the next generation.

STROKE (see BRAIN DISEASES, p. 158)

ULCERS

An ulcer is a sore which may, or may not be painful.

Mouth ulcers are common and usually clear up quite quickly. Ulcers elsewhere in the body can be more persistent.

Leg ulcers

Old people often suffer from leg ulcers, which can be very painful and very distressing. They are not dangerous, but are often difficult to clear up.

They usually start because of poor circulation to the skin of the leg. The treatment is to rest the leg, and keep the ulcer clean until healing occurs. This takes a long time.

Peptic ulcers

These can be gastric (i.e in the stomach) or duodenal (i.e. in the duodenum). It is very unusual to get one before the age of twenty. People who drink a lot of alcohol, smoke heavily and worry constantly are especially likely to get one.

An ulcer forms when, for some reason, the lining of the stomach becomes raw. Acid and digestive juices in the stomach then stop this sore area getting better. Most people suffer occasionally from indigestion. But if you have an ulcer you will probably have constant indigestion, which gets progressively worse.

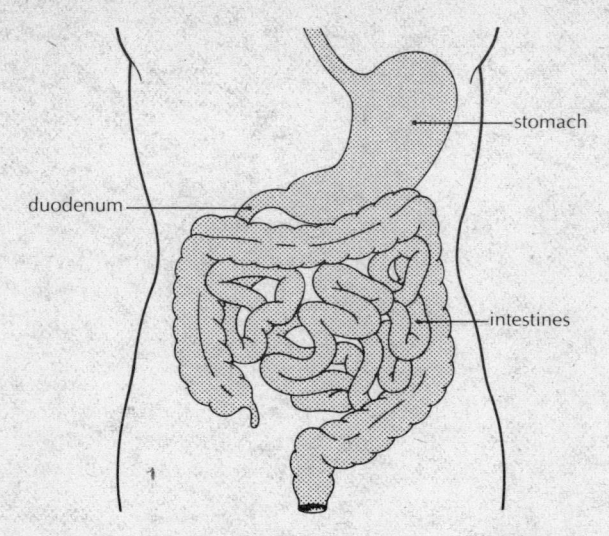

Ulcers can start either in the stomach or in the duodenum

Modern treatment for ulcers is very effective, and an operation to remove an ulcer is seldom needed. Tablets will usually clear up the trouble.

Finding out for certain whether you have an ulcer is not always easy. Often, you will be given a barium meal, which is a special X-ray (see p. 180) that outlines ulcers in the stomach. The barium liquid tastes a bit sickly, but not nasty, and having an X-ray is just like being photographed.

Gastroscopy (or endoscopy) is less pleasant. You will be given an injection to put you half-asleep, and a flexible telescope will then be put down your throat so that the doctor can look into your stomach. But because of the effects of the injection you will probably remember little of what happens to you.

8
Health Services

The health services provide advice and help about all health problems. Your family doctor will be able to advise you about most things. If he feels you need specialist advice he will know where you can get it.

But if you have a problem that for some reason you do not want to discuss with your doctor, it may help to talk to someone with particular knowledge of that problem. Under the heading HELPFUL ORGANISATIONS (see p. 181) you will find a list of alternative sources of advice.

Your family doctor

Your family doctor is the best person to consult for almost all health problems. Your local casualty department will not be pleased to see you with a trivial complaint – although it is of course quite right to go there after a serious accident. Remember that hospital doctors are very busy with other patients, so you will often have to wait to see a doctor in hospital. The senior nurse in casualty will bring a doctor quickly if you are an emergency!

If necessary, your family doctor will arrange for you to see a specialist or to have hospital treatment. If you have a problem which needs expert attention, your local hospital may send you to another hospital which specialises in the illness or injury you have.

All hospitals have many departments. They are large confusing places. Do not be afraid to ask for help if you get lost. Even doctors have been known to get lost in hospitals!

ALTERNATIVE TYPES OF MEDICINE

Conventional doctors are not the only type of health worker who can cure medical problems.

Osteopaths, who are expert at manipulating backs and curing back-ache, and acupuncture specialists who insert needles into certain parts of the body to relieve pain, are just two examples of specialists who may be able to help patients more than conventional doctors.

Homeopathic medicine, which uses natural substances to mimic illnesses, thus helping the body to cure itself, is a well-established science.

Herbalists use plants and herbs to treat certain types of illness.

BLOOD DONATING

Most blood transfusions given in the West come from volunteers. Without them, men, women and children would die every day in major accidents, during operations and as a result of blood diseases.

Anybody over the age of eighteen can give blood. Telephone your local hospital and they will tell you the time of the clinic. It is probably best to go with a friend the first time.

When you go to the clinic, the doctor will do a simple blood test (see below) to check you are fit enough to give blood. Then you will lie on a couch and a doctor will draw off one pint from a vein in your arm. This does you no harm at all. You will usually be rewarded with tea and a biscuit for your bravery!

A few unpleasant minutes for you can help save a life — every time you go.

BLOOD TESTS

A doctor may do a blood test to help him find out what is wrong with you. He will put an elastic strap round your upper arm, and then take a sample of blood from a vein in your arm with a syringe. The blood will be analysed in a laboratory.

There are many different kinds of blood test. One will find out if you are anaemic (see ANAEMIA, p. 11). Others check whether your kidneys or liver are working efficiently or whether you have had an infection. There are also special tests for glandular fever (see p. 37) and for german measles (see p. 37).

Nobody likes blood tests. But they are often necessary if the right treatment is to be given.

CLINICS

Antenatal clinics

During pregnancy, it is very important to go to a clinic regularly. This is especially true if the pregnancy is your first. Every baby deserves the best possible start in life.

The clinic checks that the unborn baby is growing well and that the mother is not becoming anaemic (see ANAEMIA, p. 11) or developing blood pressure trouble. Both these problems are easily treated, but if neglected can harm the baby.

Parents are also told what to expect at the birth and how to prepare for the baby.

Family planning clinics

These clinics give free contraceptive advice to anyone. If possible, try to book an appointment before you go. The number is in the telephone book under 'Family planning'. Most large health centres have clinics, and the doctors are often women.

There is no age qualification for visiting one of these clinics and the advice given is absolutely confidential. But if you decide to go on the contraceptive pill, the clinic will inform your doctor for health reasons, unless you strongly object.

The clinics also do pregnancy tests. They are a good place to go if you are worried that you might be pregnant.

Hospital clinics

Most hospital clinics, held in the outpatient departments of hospitals, are specialist clinics. This means that the doctor in charge specialises in one type of medicine. All his or her patients have the same sort of problem.

There are clinics for every sort of trouble — heart trouble, kidney trouble, knee or ankle trouble, period problems — you name it — there is a clinic for it. There are even special clinics for deep-sea divers and ballet dancers!

Your own doctor will usually deal with most of these problems, but if he or she wants specialist advice or if you need hospital treatment, you may well be sent to one of these clinics.

Special clinics (VD clinics)

Special clinics are clinics which deal with sexually transmitted diseases. Your family doctor or local family planning clinic has a lot of experience in these problems, but some people prefer to go straight to a hospital clinic.

If you think that you have caught an infection, get treatment or advice straight away. Treatments are simple. But if left untreated, the more serious infections can spread and cause troubles which are much harder to cure.

You can find out the address of your nearest special clinic by telephoning the local hospital. Remember to find out when the clinic is open. You do not need an appointment, and nobody is told about your visit without your permission.

Well baby clinics (developmental clinics)
These are to check up on the health and progress of newborn babies. The midwife or health visitor arranges for new mothers to attend them.

DOCTORS

Doctors come in all shapes and sizes. Like anybody else, they can be pleasant or unpleasant. But even if they seem rather frightening, remember that they would not be doctors if they did not enjoy helping others. Most doctors like seeing young people, and are usually glad to help.

Family doctors (general practitioners, or GPs, as they are known) are good at detecting serious illness and making sure that it is properly treated, if necessary in hospital. But most complaints, although troublesome, do in fact get better with simple treatment and with time. Family doctors are usually good at giving simple practical advice, especially about emotional and family problems.

If you do not like your family doctor, or want to change doctors because you are moving, simply take your medical card to the receptionist of another doctor and ask to be put on their list. If you have any difficulty, write to your local family practitioner committee, whose address is in the telephone book, and tell them that you want to change doctors.

To become a doctor, you have to be prepared to study for many years. After getting good A levels and being accepted at a teaching hospital, you will be a medical student for five years. Your family doctor or hospital specialist will have studied and gained experience as a junior hospital doctor for at least four years.

HEALTH VISITOR

A health visitor is a senior qualified nurse. Her job is to

visit new mothers and other people who need advice about health. She is particularly concerned with young children and is an expert on babies' diets and the problems that affect children under five.

She becomes a friend to many people, both young and old, who do not need a doctor but who are grateful for timely advice. The local health centre or doctor's surgery is able to put anybody in touch with her.

HOSPITALS

There are many different types of hospital. Most large towns have a district hospital with a casualty department. If you need to go to hospital this is probably where you will be taken.

Some illnesses are best treated by an expert who may work at another hospital. This specialist may be based at a teaching hospital, where student doctors are taught. Your interesting spots may be looked at by lots of young doctors!

Some hospitals specialise in one type of problem. There are eye hospitals, children's hospitals, mental health hospitals — the list is a long one.

IMMUNISATION AND VACCINATION (see also TROPICAL DISEASES, p. 57)

Immunisation and vaccination mean almost the same thing. In both cases an injection is given to protect you against a particular disease, or diseases. If you are going abroad, you may have to be immunised before you go.

Diseases such as polio, diptheria, whooping cough, tetanus, measles and tuberculosis used to kill large numbers of people. And because thousands of people had these diseases, doctors had very little time to look after other types of illness.

Nowadays, partly because of the success of immunisation campaigns, all these diseases are rarer. In fact smallpox no longer exists.

However, the protection by immunisation may not last for ever. Tetanus booster injections in particular, are needed at least every ten years. This is important if you get a bad cut, or do a job where you are likely to rub dirt into small cuts in your skin.

NURSE

Most nurses work in hospitals or clinics. District nurses work closely with family doctors and nurse people at home when necessary.

Nurses, both men and women, are usually dedicated people. The pay is not good and the work is often hard. Almost all nurses who take a lot of responsibility have a state registered qualification, which requires three years of studying after leaving school. Less well qualified nurses have considerable practical experience, but are less likely to be promoted.

The senior nurse on a hospital ward is called the sister. She and the doctor are in charge of the ward together. If you are in hospital, she will be able to answer any questions you have about your treatment and how long you can expect to stay.

OPERATION

It is always a bit frightening going into hospital for an operation, though nowadays even quite big operations are very safe.

You will probably be asked to come to the hospital the day before the operation, unless the operation is an emergency. You will often have a blood test (see p. 173) and sometimes an X-ray (see p. 180). This is to check that you do not need extra treatment before the operation.

You will then be taken to a ward and given a bed. Even though it may still be day-time, you will be asked to undress and get in. Make sure you take some books or games into hospital with you to pass the time.

About an hour before the operation time, a nurse will come to help you get ready for the operation. You will need to wash and put on a special gown. She will then give you an injection.

This injection, called a premed, makes you sleepy, so that you are only vaguely aware of being put on a trolley and taken to the operating theatre. A doctor will then give you another injection in the back of the hand to put you to sleep. You will hardly notice it. The doctor giving the anaesthetic may ask you to breathe pure oxygen through a mask. This makes the anaesthetic a little pleasanter, although some people dislike the mask.

The next thing you know you will be back in your bed and the operation will be over. You will be stiff and sore. You may feel a bit sick. A nurse may give you a painkilling injection so that you sleep again.

The following day you will wake up properly. You will still feel a bit sore, and will probably still want regular painkillers. But the worst is over.

By the second day, you will be on the mend. Any stitches you have will stay in for about a week, unless they are self-dissolving stitches which do not need taking out.

How long you stay in hospital after an operation depends on the type of operation. For example, if you have your wisdom teeth out, you will probably stay one night; the removal of your adenoids or tonsils will mean three to five nights; and an appendicectomy (having your appendix removed) five to seven nights.

Minor operations

Smaller operations can be done under local anaesthetic. With these a stay in hospital is not necessary.

The area is numbed by an injection, which stings briefly, although it does help if you keep still. During the operation you should not feel any pain, although you may feel tense and uncomfortable.

Both dentists and hospital casualty departments frequently use local anaesthetic to relieve the pain of extracting teeth and stitching up cuts.

PHYSIOTHERAPY

Physiotherapy is a type of treatment, usually arranged at hospital, which aims to get your limbs moving again after an accident or illness. The special exercises that physiotherapists teach also help with chest infections.

Physiotherapists use modern equipment to speed up recovery in the treatment of sporting injuries. This equipment warms or stimulates the injured muscles.

SOCIAL WORKER

Social workers carry out a great variety of jobs, many of which should, ideally, be done by relatives or friendly neighbours. For example, old people may need a social worker to sort out difficulties over a pension; young people in trouble with the police may be helped by a social worker to get the problem ironed out in the fairest possible way.

Social workers also provide special services for the mentally ill and handicapped – helping them to cope outside hospital.

Social workers will also help if you are homeless, or have some other problem you feel unable to cope with. But remember that they are extremely busy people and do not want to become involved if it is not necessary. But if you feel completely unable to cope, you can get an appointment with a social worker at your local social services department.

X-RAY

An X-ray machine takes pictures of the body which show the outline of the bones. X-rays are a great help in deciding if a bone is cracked or broken. But a doctor will not always order an X-ray after an injury. An X-ray does not actually cure anything, and a careful examination will often tell a doctor all he needs to know.

Routine X-rays of girls should always be done just after the start of her period. Otherwise, there is a risk she might be pregnant and X-rays can (very occasionally) harm a growing baby.

Very large X-ray machines, which give a three-dimensional picture, are called scanners. They are very useful in the detection of cancers and other serious diseases. However, they are extremely expensive both to buy and to operate.

X-ray treatment

X-rays are also used in the treatment of certain types of cancer (see p. 159). When X-rays are shone on them, they shrivel up and die. This treatment is called Deep X-ray Therapy (DXT).

Helpful Organisations

If you are in trouble and need help, go to a relative, teacher or youth leader you can trust and ask them for their advice. Doctors, priests and clergymen will also listen and give advice absolutely confidentially. Health visitors will probably be able to give help with any problem involving a child under the age of five.

If you feel you cannot ask for advice from anyone you know, you can always approach an organisation, such as one of those listed below. You will find their telephone numbers and addresses in the telephone directory. Otherwise, call in at your local social services office and ask to see a duty social worker.

The larger the city or town in which you live, the more likely it is to have the following organisations.

Aged relatives	Age Concern
Alcohol problems	Alcoholics Anonymous
Children, violence and neglect	NSPCC
Contraception and pregnancy	Brook Advisory centres, Family Planning Association
Desperation, feeling suicidal	Samaritan's telephone service
Food, noise and pest complaints	Environmental health services
Housing problems	Social services
	Voluntary groups (get addresses from public library)

Legal problems	Citizens Advice Bureau and Legal Advice Centres
Relationship problems	Marriage Guidance councils (they will advise single people!)
Special situations	Local councillor or MP
Venereal disease	(see CLINICS, p. 174)

Other organisations

Asthma – The Chest, Heart and Stroke Association, Tavistock House North, Tavistock Square, London WC1H 9JE

Deafness – National Deaf Children's Society, 45 Hereford Road, London W2

Diabetes – British Diabetic Association, 10 Queen Anne Street, London W1N OBD

Epilepsy – British Epilepsy Association, New Wokingham Road, Wokingham, Berkshire

Handicap – Voluntary Council for Handicapped Children, 8 Wakely Street London EC1

Further reading

Chapter 1. General Health
THE BODY, Anthony Smith (Penguin, 1970)
   Useful background book on all aspects of human biology and social implications
THE BODY AND HEALTH, Brian Ward (MacDonald 'Guidelines', 1976) Detailed look at body functions and keeping healthy
EVERYTHING YOUR DOCTOR WOULD TELL YOU IF HE HAD TIME, Clare Rayner (Pan, 1979) Presented in a question and answer format with clear diagrams
MANS BODY: AN OWNERS MANUAL (Corgi, 1981)
   A clear, diagrammatic account of bodily functions
OUR BODIES, OURSELVES, Angela Philips and Jill Rakusen (Penguin, 1980)
   A handbook by and for women on all aspects of women's health
WOMANS BODY: AN OWNERS MANUAL (Corgi, 1981)
   A clear, diagrammatic account of bodily functions

Chapter 3. Food, Diet and Growth
EAT WELL AND KEEP HEALTHY, Merrill Durrant (MacDonald 'Guidelines')
   A book on all aspects of diet and nutrition. Contains many charts, pictures and diagrams
FOOD, Richard Mabey (Penguin)
   Food ingredients, marketing and social customs are investigated by cartoons, photography, news clippings

Chapter 4. Drugs and Medicines
DRUGS, Peter Laurie (Penguin)
  Survey of most drugs, including alcohol
STOP! (Penguin)
  A guide to stopping smoking

Chapter 5. Personal Relationships and Mental Health
CHILD CARE, Ann Burkitt (Nelson, 1975)
  Well illustrated workbook on child development and parentcraft which requires an advanced reading age
CHILD CARE, Graeme Snodgrass (MacDonald 'Guidelines', 1978) Comprehensive, adult guide to child development with graphs, charts and photographs
UNDERSTANDING YOUR BABY, Dorothy Baldwin (Ebury Press, 1975)
  Pupils book for parents-to-be covering child development from birth to the age of 3, with photographs, drawings and strip cartoons depicting typical family situations

Chapter 6. Sex
MAKE IT HAPPY, Jane Cousins (Virago, 1978; Penguin 1980)
  A directory of sexuality for young people
HAVE YOU STARTED YET?, Ruth Thomson (Heinemann and Piccolo, 1980)
  Girls' experiences are used to discuss all aspects of menstruation

Index

Numbers in **bold** type indicate main headings

Abortion, **145**
Abscess, **9**
Achondroplasia, 82
Acne, **61**
Addiction, **91**
Adenoids, 30
Adolescence, **105**
AIDS, 149
Albino, 73
Alcohol, 92, **93**
Alcoholism, 92, **94**
Allergy, **9**, 74
Alopecia, 69
Amphetamines, 96
Anaemia, **11**
Angina, 165
Ankylosing spondylitis, 13
Anorexia nervosa, **79**
Antenatal clinic, 139, 173
Antibiotic, **95**
Antidepressant, 95
Antihistamine, **96**
Antral washout, 31
Appearance, 61, 114
Appendicitis, **11**, 49, 177
Artery disease, **154**
Arthritis, **13, 155**
Asthma, **59**
Athletes foot, 63

Back, 13, **15**, 88
Bacteria, **41**
Bad breath, **15**
Balanced diet, **80**
Barbiturates, 97
BCG Injection, 58
Bedwetting, **15**
Birth, 127, **140**
Black eye, 17
Bleeding, **16**
Blisters, **64**
Blocked nose, 47
Blood donating, **172**

Blood poisoning, 156
Blood pressure, **157**
Blood test, 11, **173**
Blushing, **64**
Body odour, **65**
Boils, **65**
Breasts, 124, 126, 131
Breathing, 43
Broken bone, **35**
Broken nose, 47
Bronchitis, **17**, 43
Bruising, **17**
Bullying, 118
Bunions, **18**
Burns, **18**

Caesarian section, 141
Calory, **79**
Cancer, **159**
Cannabis, 97
Carbohydrate, **80**
Carbuncle, **9**
Cartilage, 14
Cataract, 33
Chickenpox, **19**
Chilblains, **66**
Childbirth, 127, **140**
Cholera, 58
Circulation of blood, **20**
Cirrhosis, 94
Clinics, **173**
Cocaine, 97
Coeliac disease, 11
Colds, **21**
Cold sores, **66**
Colitis, **160**
Colour blindness, 33
Concussion, **21**
Conjunctivitis, 31
Constipation, **22**
Contact lens, 32
Contraception, **142**

185

Convulsion, 34
Corns, **66**
Cough, **23**
Cramp, **23**
Crohns disease, 161
Croup, **23**
Cuts, **24**
Cystic fibrosis, **24**
Cystitis, **25**

Dandruff, **67**
Deafness, **30**
Deficiencies (diet), 86, 89
Depression, 95, 110
Dermatitis, 74
Diabetes, **26**, 103, 162
Diarrhoea, **27**, 160
Dieting, **81, 87**
Dislocation, **28**
Doctors, 171, **175**
Double joints, 28
Downs syndrome, **28**
Drug abuse, **96**
Drunkenness, 93
Dwarves, **82**

Ear, **29**
Earache, **29**
Ear piercing, **67**
Eczema, **68**
Epilepsy, 34
Eye, **31**

Fainting, **55**
Family, **106**
Family planning, 142, 173
Fatigue, **55**
Fats, **82**
Fever, **33**
Fibre, **82**
Fingernails, 71
Fits, **34**
Flu, 13, **35**
Fluoride, 55
Food hygiene, **83**
Food poisoning, 83
Food storage, **84**
Forceps birth, 141
Fractures, **35**
Freckles, **68**

Gallstones, **161**
Genital warts, 149
German measles, 13, **37**
Gigantism, 85
Giving blood, **172**
Glands, 162

Glandular fever, **37**
Glasses, 32
Glue sniffing, 98
Gonorrhoea, 148
Gout, 155
Grommets, 31

Haemophilia, 18
Hair, **68**
Halitosis, **15**
Hay fever, 10, **38**
Headache, **38**
Head injury, 21
Heaf test, 58
Health visitor, 175
Heart, 20, **163**
Heartburn, 39
Height, **85**
Helpful organisations, **181**
Henoch-schoenlein, 18
Hepatitis, 42
Hernia, **39**
Heroin, 92, 97
Herpes, 149
Hip, 13, 155
Hole in heart, 164
Homosexuality, 150
Hormones, 162
Hospitals, 171, 174, **176**, 177
Hypertension, 157
Hypo (diabetes), 26

Immunisation, **176**
Indigestion, **39**, 168
Infection, **41**, 95
Influenza, **35**
Insulin, 26
Intelligence, 116
Iron tablets, 11
Irritable bowel, 161
Irritable hip, 13
Itching, **70**

Jaundice, **42**
Job application, 115

Keloid, 75
Kidney disease, **166**
Knee, 14, 53

Laryngitis, **43**
Laxatives, 22
Legionnaires disease, 57
Leprosy, 57
Leukaemia, 156
Lice, **70**, 149
Ligaments, 15
Liver, 42, 94

LSD, 98
Lumbar puncture, 46
Lungs, **43**

Madness, 111
Malaria, 57
Malnutrition, **86**
Mania, 112
Mastoid operation, 31
Masturbation, **133**
Measles, 37, **45**, 176
Meningitis, **45**
Menstruation, 129
Mental handicap, **109**
Mental illness, **109**
Migraine, 38, **46**
Moles, **71**
Mongolism, 28
Motion sickness, 50
Multiple sclerosis, 159
Mumps, **46**
Muscular dystrophy, 47

Nailbiting, 73
Nails, **71**
Nettlerash, 74
Neurosis, 110
Nose, **47**
Nosebleeds, 16
Nurse, 175, **177**

Old age, 112, **114**, 153
Operation, 13, 30, **177**
Osteoarthritis, 155
Osteochondritis, 13
Overdose, 99
Overweight, **86**
Ovulation, 129

Parents, 106
Parkinsons disease, 159
Penicillin, 95
Periods, 129
Peritonitis, **48**
Personality, 114
Perthes disease, 14
Phobia, 111
Physical handicap, **167**
Physiotherapy, **179**
Pigmentation, 73
Plaque, **54**
Pleurisy, 44
Pneumonia, 44
Pneumothorax, 45
Posture, **88**
Pregnancy, **137**

Pregnancy test, 139
Protein, **89**
Psoriasis, **73**
Psychosis, 111
Puberty, **132**
Pubic lice, 149
Pus, 9

Rash, 9, **74**
Rheumatoid arthritis, 156
Rhinitis, 48
Rickets, 86
Ringworm, **74**
Roughage, **82**
Rubella, 37

Scabies, **75**
Scalds, 18
Scarring, **75**
Scheurmanns disease, 13
Schizophrenia, 112
School, **117**
Scurvy, 86
Seborrheic dermatitis, 67
Sedatives, 98, **100**
Senility, 113
Sexuality, 105, 116, 134, 149
Sexual intercourse, **135**
Sexual relationships, **118**
Sexual organs
    male, **121**
    female, **124**
Sexually transmitted diseases, **147**, 174
Shingles, 20
Shock, **49**
Shyness, 116
Sickle-cell disease, 156
Sickness, **50**
Side-effect, **101**
Sight, 31
Sinusitis, **51**
Skin, **61**
Skin grafting, 19
Sleeping pills, **101**
Slipped disc, 15
Slipped epiphysis, 14
Smallpox, 57
Smoking, 92, **102**
Smear test, 131
Social worker, **179**
Sore throat, **51**
Spina bifida, 167
Spots, 61
Sprain, **52**
Squint, 32
Stammer, **53**
STD, **147**, 174
Steroids, **101**

187

Stomach ache, **53**
Stroke, 158
Stye, 32
Subconscious, **119**
Sugar, 80
Suicide, 99
Sunburn, **75**
Sunstroke, 75
Syphilis, 148

Tattooing, **76**
Teeth, 54
Tetanus, 24, 176
Threadworms, 60
Thrush, 148
Thyroid, 162
Thyroxin, 162
Tiredness, **55**
Tobacco, 92, **102**
Toenails, 72
Tonsilitis, 13, **56**
Toothache, 55
Tranquillisers, 98, 100
Travel sickness, 50
Tropical diseases, **57**
Tuberculosis, **58**, 176
Typhoid, 58

Ulcers, **168**

Urethritis, 148
Urine infection, **24**

Vaccination, **176**
Vaginal infections, 148
Varicose veins, 59
Veins, **58**
Venereal disease, **147**
Verruca, **76**
Vertebra, 15
Virus infection, **41**
Vitamins, **89**
Vitiligo, 73
Vomiting, **50**

Warts, **76**, 149
Weight, 86, **89**
Wheezing, 10, **59**
Whitlow, **77**
Whooping cough, **60**, 176
Worms, **60**
Wounds, 24

X-ray, **180**

Yellow fever, 42, 58

On the following pages you will find some other exciting Beaver book titles for you to look out for in your local bookshop.

BODY MAGIC
Peter Eldin

A collection of amazing stunts, tricks and activities designed to help you understand the delicate machinery that makes up the human body. There are optical illusions which the reader can try which show how the eyes and brain function; also balancing skills, tests of touch and so on. There are also some pretty extraordinary facts. Few people know, for instance, that a piece of skin the size of a 5p coin contains over three million cells, one hundred sweat glands and twenty-five nerve endings or that we have about 100,000 hairs on our heads or that a young person has more bones than an old.

If you're an eager Beaver reader, perhaps you ought to try some more of our exciting titles. They are available in bookshops or they can be ordered directly from us. Just complete the form below and enclose the right amount of money and the books will be sent to you at home.

THE BEAVER BOOK OF MAGIC	Gyles Brandreth	95p ☐
MR ENIGMA'S CODE MYSTERIES	Tim Healey	95p ☐
THE HORROR'S HANDBOOK	Eric Kenneway	95p ☐
THE RUBBER BAND BOOK	Eric Kenneway	£1.00 ☐
CAN PLANTS TALK?	Ralph Levinson	£1.00 ☐
HOW TO MAKE SQUARE EGGS	Paul Temple and Ralph Levinson	£1.00 ☐
THE BEAVER BOOK OF FOOTBALL	Tom Tully	60p ☐
AN A-Z OF MONSTERS	Ian Woodward	95p ☐
THE BEAVER HOLIDAY QUIZ	Robin May	85p ☐
THE BEAVER BOOK OF BRAIN TICKLERS	Charles Booth Jones	85p ☐
THE BEAVER BOOK OF TONGUE TWISTERS	Janet Rogers	80p ☐

And if you would like to hear more about Beaver Books, and find out all the latest news, don't forget the BEAVER BULLETIN. If you just send a stamped self-addressed envelope to Beaver Books, 17-21 Conway Street, LONDON W1P 6JD, we will send you one.

If you would like to order books, please send this form, and the money due to:

HAMLYN PAPERBACK CASH SALES, PO BOX 11, FALMOUTH, CORNWALL, TR10 9EN.

Send a cheque or postal order, and don't forget to include postage at the following rates: UK: 45p for the first book, 20p for second, 14p thereafter to a maximum of £1.63; BFPO and Eire: 45p for first book, 20p for second, 14p per copy for next 7 books, 8p per book thereafter; Overseas: 75p for first book, 21p thereafter.

NAME..

ADDRESS...

....
PLEASE PRINT CLEARLY